NEW LIFE

NEW LIFE

An Anthology for Parenthood

Edited by Sally Emerson

Little, Brown

LITTLE, BROWN

First published in Great Britain as a paperback original
in 2009 by Little, Brown

A CIP catalogue record for this book
is available from the British Library.

ISBN 978-1-4087-0112-6

Typeset in Bembo by M Rules
Printed and bound in Great Britain by Clays Ltd, St Ives plc

Papers used by Little, Brown are natural, renewable and recyclable
products sourced from well-managed forests and certified
in accordance with the rules of the Forest Stewardship Council.

Mixed Sources
Product group from well-managed
forests and other controlled sources
www.fsc.org Cert no. SGS-COC-004081
© 1996 Forest Stewardship Council

FSC

Little, Brown
An imprint of
Little, Brown Book Group
100 Victoria Embankment
London EC4Y 0DY

An Hachette UK Company
www.hachette.co.uk

www.littlebrown.co.uk

To Anna and Michael

CONTENTS

Cℨ

BIRTH

𝄢

NAMINGS AND BLESSINGS

Mother Love

✵

FATHER LOVE

GAMES TO PLAY WITH BABIES

A NEW VOICE

ः

SLEEPY LOVE SONGS

✹

ADVICE AND SAYINGS

✹

FAMILIES

✿

A WORLD OF THEIR OWN

INTRODUCTION

'Keep still while I'm trying to levitate you,' demanded my six-year-old daughter as I lay on the kitchen table. 'Stop giggling.' Ah, it has been magic, the whole zig-zagging, wild journey of being a parent.

This anthology explores the wonder of a new child and the new life a child brings to the family, as well as the reality of new fears and responsibilities. As John Fuller writes in 'Birth Bells for Louisa', 'Time now makes a new beginning'.

Cynicism, world weariness and despair all left me on the day of my first child's birth and have only made casual appearances in my life since. Time certainly made a new beginning for me.

It is the high-spirited comedy of life with young children that is perhaps the greatest joy; the daily epiphanies when you think life just could not possibly get any better or more utterly, wonderfully ridiculous – my daughter hanging upside down from the bed as she learnt the spelling of the word 'ran'. Upside down 'so the spelling stays in', she kept sliding down on to the floor and her cherubic younger brother and I kept laughing. He always seemed to be laughing. He followed her, as Deborah Garrison writes, down 'babyhood's brief corridor'. Forget wealth, fame, all that, just give me those moments of glee.

Garrison writes carefully about families, brothers and sisters, as does Sharon Olds, whose splendid poems so tenderly dissect the ravages of this love.

New Life explores the new life a baby brings and the new way of living a family creates: conception; pregnancy; birth; pieces for namings and blessings; the joy of a new baby; mother love; father love; family tensions; advice and sayings; and the pleasure in watching and listening to a new voice in this old world. Here too are games to play with babies, and lullabies to rock them to sleep, from John Lennon's 'Beautiful Boy' to a little-known Armenian song.

I have tried not to let my own enthusiasm push out the other side of the story: the sorrows and the difficulties; the sleepless nights; the post-natal depression; the sheer hard work of dealing with a vulnerable human being twenty-four hours a day. Rachel Cusk and Kate Saunders explore the struggle of being a parent.

Pregnancy made me sick, dumped me into hospital on a drip, and birth hurt like mad both times. As Yosano Akiko wrote, 'With the first labour pains,/suddenly the sun goes pale.' Rebecca Eckler announced, 'I am never studying another pregnancy book again until I absolutely have no choice. It will be just like high school. When I start having contractions, I'll cram.'

But the point of it all is not the birth, but the baby, the new individual who turns up in your arms and demands your attention for a lifetime. In 'The Girlfriends' Guide to Surviving the First Year of Motherhood' Vicki Lovine writes that the birth of a baby is supposed to blow your schedule to bits: 'This is nature's way of making sure that we get our new priorities straight. The three most important things become, in this order 1. The baby's health. 2. The baby's comfort 3. The baby's parents survival (this is a very distant third).'

To me, from the outside, it hadn't looked great. Mothers had seemed to be odd, out-of-focus creatures, standing waiting outside schools, endlessly waiting, struggling with pushchairs. Yet once I had children I was propelled into a clear new world; I saw everything through their eyes and the world was a dramatic and miraculous place. Giacomo Leopardi wrote 'Children find everything in nothing, men find nothing in everything.'

Gurus in New York make fortunes teaching us to live in the moment but just look at the babies: they know how. And if you are with a baby you have no choice but to live in the moment. It's where they are. As Philip Lerman writes in 'How a Real Man Became a Real Dad', 'Your child is in the moment and of the moment . . . why would I want to stop playing Doll from Planet Blobby? There is no other game. This is the game.'

Baby games are about the moment; I've included some of the many traditional, joyous rhymes that delight babies, from tickling games such as 'Round and Round the Garden' and 'This Little Piggy went to Market' to more rumbustious knee rides. After all, these are games passed on through generations; they are both of the moment and belong to all time. And when you play them you have to be fully present. You cannot be thinking of anything else, of your work, or the television, or your holiday plans, because the magic doesn't work. Yes, it's eyes on their faces, watching the slow smiles of excitement erupt into giggles of delight, and the rest of the world can get lost. Here you are. There is nowhere else.

Here are lullabies too, from all over the world; love songs to babies. In the past babies and small children have been women's business and have seldom been awarded the accolade of poetry or fine writing. Oral poetry, lullabies, have been the way in which women have expressed their love. Caring for babies and children takes up immense portions of the human race's time, yet only now is there a proper body of literature developing on the subject. Look at the poems by Sylvia Plath. Her sense of wonder and respect, and her exactness, set a new tone. In 'You're' the images are both small – 'Snug as a bud' – and immense – 'Bent-backed Atlas' – and encapsulate the huge power of these relentless, tiny creatures.

Anne Ridler writes 'But the birth of a child is an uncontrollable glory', and Audre Lorde records that 'my legs were towers between which/A new world was passing.' Anne Stevenson observes in 'Poem for a Daughter', 'The child,/ Tiny and alone, creates the mother'.

This anthology aims to be a source of entertainment and solace, but it also records the extraordinary changes that have come about in our attitudes to women and to children, attitudes that are finding their voice in powerful poetry and prose, fresh and vigorous. This is a mighty time for a whole new subject, approached in a new way.

3

While the Romantics, for instance, saw children as visions of hope, the new work here by such fine writers as Carol Ann Duffy selflessly and meticulously records the nature of the child, and analyses the nature of the parent's love.

In poem after poem we see both the grandeur of babies as they arrive on this planet, and their vulnerability. Women have previously been chary of being called sentimental or gushing if they show too much enthusiasm for babies (and perhaps women have been fearful of confessing how much they love their children in case it makes men jealous and resentful). Writers such as Penelope Shuttle can now proclaim how 'delicious' babies are, without sentimentality. Joyce Carol Oates, in 'Foetal Song', writes of a child 'waiting' for 'my turn', and Sharon Olds of being 'nothing, no one, I was everything to her, I was hers'.

Now poets such as Anne Ridler, Judith Wright and Anne Stevenson have a penetrating, often ruthlessly detailed, take on an area of living that has been strangely ignored for so long. The outburst of new poetry, new prose – puzzled, amazed, enraptured – is all just the beginning.

The great canon of British poetry includes few poems about babies, though of course there are sublime poems such as Coleridge's 'Frost at Midnight' which capture the stillness and intimacy of nighttime with a new baby. Coleridge is one of the few major writers of the past to write about babies and young children with real gaiety and joy, as if the writing is about them rather than about him.

Of course, babies used to be strictly women's business and the experience of raising children considered hardly worthy of prose, let alone poetry. As men have begun to take an interest in babies the status of the subject has increased and women as well as men now feel birth and babies are significant enough subjects for literature. Sylvia Plath does not write about the baby as a future adult or as a Romantic symbol of innocence, but as a glorious infant. The baby's 'moth-breath/Flickers among the flat pink roses'.

In the course of researching this anthology I found extraordinary poets who were unknown to me. Jeni Couzyn mixes simplicity with startling images as she takes a voyage in words around her baby's lovely body, referring to the ear as a 'tiny sea-horse', the mouth as 'a foxglove in its taking/Without edges or hurt'. Look out also for the work of the little-known poet, E. J. (Edith Joy) Scovell (1907–1999), with her image of a baby rising on its hands like a mermaid from its sea of blankets.

Here and there in the past you can find strong writing by women on babies, though no doubt much was written but not published and some poems published but then neglected. Now the re-evaluation of women's writing and the experience of women is beginning to find these neglected writers again. I particularly like Anna Lætitia Barbauld's poem from the eighteenth century 'To a little Invisible Being Who Is Expected Soon to Become Visible', and Augusta Webster (1837–94) on how her daughter is 'Loverlike', continuously noting her mother's beauty: 'And I forget to age, through her sweet will.' Her, too, are Mrs Gaskell's detailed diaries about her children and poems by the childless Christina Rossetti.

In the oral tradition the passion has long come through. The best lullabies, whether made up by unknown tribal women or by John Lennon, are love songs crooned to soothe the babies and persuade them not to be afraid, to lull the fear of the darkness and to help them fall asleep: 'Close your eyes,/Have no fear,/The monster's gone,/He's on the run and your daddy's here,/Beautiful,/Beautiful, beautiful,/Beautiful boy.' A lullaby from the Lebanon sings that 'A blanket are my eye-lashes/Woven for thee.' An Armenian lullaby romantically murmurs 'How lovely you are, you seem to have no flaws?/What shall I bring which is as flawless . . . Let me go and fetch the moon,/The flawless moon and the stars.'

The intellectual joys of raising children is touched on here and there, by such writers as A. S. Byatt in 'A New Voice' from *Still Life*. After all, what could be more interesting than seeing humanity at its very beginning, before it is touched by the world's slow stain? A parent sees all this first-hand, in twenty-four-hour detail, watching day by day the impact of experiences on a particular character. What is it that we see? How does language develop, is morality instinctive, does good behaviour have to be learnt, and how is a baby altered by its experiences? New studies such as 'The Baby in the Mirror: A Child's

World from Birth to Three' by Charles Fernyhough (a parent who is also a psychologist) are beginning to chart this territory in detail.

Perhaps the greatest joy of parenthood is the love for babies and children, proper love of the purest kind. Laurie Lee writes 'She was of course just an ordinary miracle . . . Now she was here, brand new, with our name upon her, and no one could call in the night to reclaim her.'

I was with a friend, watching her determined two-year-old daughter pour water into the ocean from a can to keep the ocean from drying out. 'She makes up for everything that's ever gone wrong in my thirty-eight years, she really does,' said my radiant friend who had been sad for so long, until she gave birth to her daughter. 'And to imagine I might have been put off because of people talking about the problems.'

JOY

Delicious Babies

Because of spring there are babies everywhere,
sweet or sulky, irascible or full of the milk of human
     kindness.
Yum, yum! Delicious babies!
Babies with the soft skins of babies, cheeks
of such tit-bit pinkness, tickle-able babies, tasty babies,
mouth-watering babies

The pads of their hands! The rounds
of their knees! Their good smells of bathtime
and new clothes and gobbled rusks!
Even their discarded nappies are worthy of them, reveal
     their powers.
Legions and hosts of babies! Babies bold as lions, sighing
     babies,
tricksy babies, omniscient babies, babies using a plain
     language
of reasonable demands and courteous acceptance.
Others have the habit of loud contradiction,
can empty a railway carriage (though their displeasing
     howls
cheer up childless women).
Look at this baby, sitting bolt upright in his buggy!
Consider his lofty unsmiling acknowledgement of our
     adulation.

Look at the elfin golfer's hat flattering his fluffy hair!
Look next at this very smallest of babies
tightly wrapped in a foppery of blankets.
In his high promenading pram he sleeps sumptuously,
only a nose, his father's, a white bonnet and a wink
of eyelid showing.

All babies are manic–serene, all babies are mine,
all babies are edible, the boys taste best.
I feed on them, nectareous are my babies,
manna, confiture, my sweet groceries.

I smack my lips,
deep in my belly the egg ripens,
makes the windows shake,
another ovum-quake
moves earth, sky and me . . .

Bring me more babies! Let me have them for breakfast,
lunch and tea! Let me feast, let my honey-banquet of babies
go on forever, fresh deliveries night and day!

PENELOPE SHUTTLE (1947–)

You're

Clownlike, happiest on your hands,
Feet to the stars, and moon-skulled,
Gilled like a fish. A common-sense
Thumbs-down on the dodo's mode.
Wrapped up in yourself like a spool,
Trawling your dark as owls do.
Mute as a turnip from the Fourth
Of July to All Fools' Day,
O high-riser, my little loaf.

Vague as fog and looked for like mail.
Farther off than Australia.
Bent-backed Atlas, our traveled prawn.
Snug as a bud and at home
Like a sprat in a pickle jug
A creel of eels, all ripples.
Jumpy as a Mexican bean.
Right, like a well-done sum.
A clean slate, with your own face on.

SYLVIA PLATH (1932–63)

Firstborn

And she brought forth her firstborn son, and wrapped him in swaddling clothes, and laid him in a manger, because there was no room for them in the inn . . .

St Luke 2: 7

To Miss Charlotte Pulteney
in Her Mother's Arms

Timely blossom, infant fair,
Fondling of a happy pair,
Every morn and every night,
Their solicitous delight,
Sleeping, waking, still at ease,
Pleasing, without skill to please,
Little gossip, blithe and hale,
Tattling many a broken tale,
Singing many a tuneless song,
Lavish of a heedless tongue,
Simple maiden void of art,
Babbling out the very heart,
Yet abandoned to thy will,
Yet imagining no ill,
Yet too innocent to blush,
Like the linlet in the bush,
To the mother-linnet's note
Moduling her slender throat,
Chirping forth thy petty joys,
Wanton in the change of toys,
Like the linnet green in May,
Flitting to each bloomy spray,
Wearied then, and glad of rest,
Like the linlet in the nest
This thy present happy lot,
This, in time, will be forgot:
Other pleasures, other cares,
Ever-busy time prepares;
And thou shalt in thy daughter see
This picture, once, resembled thee.

AMBROSE PHILIPS (*c.*1675–1749)

Navajo Chant

I have made a baby board for you my daughter
May you grow to a great old age
Of the sun's rays I have made the back
Of black clouds I have made the blanket
Of rainbow I have made the bow
Of sunbeams I have made the side loops
Of lightning I have made the lacings
Of raindrops have I made the footboard,
Of dawn have I made the bed covering . . .

TRADITIONAL

from Birth Bells for Louisa

TIME NOW MAKES A NEW BEGINNING

Time now makes a new beginning.
The world is both outside and inside.
  Live with our love.

At this moment there is no past
And consciousness is everywhere.
  Live with our love.

The world is both outside and inside
And now the worlds must be united.
  Live with our love.

And consciousness is everywhere
Of newly integrated spaces.
  Live with our love.

And now the worlds must be united
Into a manifold of being.
  Live with our love.

Of newly integrated spaces
What shall we say except that they
  Live with our love?

Into a manifold of being
Time now makes its new beginning.
  Live with our love, with our love.

JOHN FULLER (1937–)

PREGNANCY

The Conceiving

for Zoe

Now
you are in the ark of my blood
in the river of my bones
in the woodland of my muscles
in the ligaments of my hair
in the wit of my hands
in the smear of my shadow
in the armada of my brain
under the stars of my skull
in the arms of my womb
Now you are here
you worker in the gold of flesh

PENELOPE SHUTTLE (1947–)

Freight

I am the ship in which you sail,
little dancing bones,
your passage between the dream
and the waking dream,
your sieve, your pea-green boat.
I'll pay whatever toll your ferry needs.
And you, whose history's already charted
in a rope of cells, be tender to
those other unnamed vessels
who will surprise you one day,
tug-tugging, irresistible,
and float you out beyond your depth,
where you'll look down, puzzled, amazed.

MAURA DOOLEY (1957–)

Knocked Up

27 Jan
How could I have been so stupid? I have ruined my life. I am never having sex again. I mean, I am never having unprotected sex again. Unprotected sex, like that black dress I wore the other night, is a bad idea. Ten minutes of great sex and my life is over. But another life has just begun. Life apparently does not happen when you're busy making other plans. Life is what happens when there is an open bar.

4 Feb
What are the chances that one itty-bitty sperm, one 1,000th of an inch long, managed to strike my egg at just the right angle, at just the right time? Make that, what are the chances that one itty-bitty *drunk* sperm, one 1,000th of an inch long, managed to strike my *drunk* egg at just the right angle, at just the right time? I could barely walk upright when we got home that night. How could the sperm possibly manage to swim straight? . . . Nah, the chances I'm pregnant are next to nil. I can't even get my VCR to work and I've had it for ten years. How is it possible that in ten minutes, without actually knowing how anything in my body works, I could be pregnant?

28 Feb
I am never studying another pregnancy book again until I absolutely have no choice. It will be just like high school. When I start having contractions, I'll cram.

REBECCA ECKLER (1973–)

Two Months Gone

It makes us want to shut all doors,
turn off the news, the phone, light
after light, pull the stairs, like a ladder,
up behind us, until, beneath the covers,
the darkness pressing around us,

we are the pair in the heart of the tale,
the woodsman who spared the unicorn,
the kitchen maid who hooked a witch
from the well and held her toe
through fourteen frightful incarnations,

and won, walked home with a wish
like a brimming glass of water, and when
the goblin with the question came,
sang out, to his single rhymed conundrum,
the answer: *all we ever wanted.*

In the black after the thunderclap, we wait
for the crooked town to wake, find
gilded roofs, loaves on each table,
for the crowds to come, half-dressed, incredulous,
for our fortune squalling in its cradle.

KATE CLANCHY (1965–)

The Sonogram
from The Prince of the Quotidian

Only a few weeks ago, the sonogram of Jean's womb
resembled nothing so much
as a satellite-map of Ireland:

now the image
is so well-defined we can make out not only a hand
but a thumb;

on the road to Spiddal, a woman hitching a ride;
a gladiator in his net, passing judgement on the crowd.

PAUL MULDOON (1951–)

from To a Little Invisible Being Who Is Expected Soon to Become Visible

For thee the nurse prepares her lulling songs,
The eager matrons count the lingering day;
But far the most thy anxious parent longs
On thy soft cheek a mother's kiss to lay.

She only asks to lay her burden down,
That her glad arms that burden may resume;
And nature's sharpest pangs her wishes crown,
That free thee living from thy living tomb.

She longs to fold to her maternal breast
Part of herself, yet to herself unknown;
To see and to salute the stranger guest,
Fed with her life through many a tedious moon.

Come, reap thy rich inheritance of love!
Bask in the fondness of a Mother's eye!
Nor wit nor eloquence her heart shall move
Like the first accents of thy feeble cry.

Haste, little captive, burst thy prison doors!
Launch on the living world, and spring to light!
Nature for thee displays her various stores,
Opens her thousand inlets of delight.

If charmèd verse or muttered prayers had power
With favouring spells to speed thee on thy way,
Anxious I'd bid my beads each passing hour,
Till thy wished smile thy mother's pangs o'erpay.

ANNA LÆTITIA BARBAULD (1743–1825)

First Kick

For every mother, the first kick of her first baby must be memorable —
as the first tangible *communication*. At that moment I was sitting on a
sun-warmed boulder in the Selijuk ruins of Ani, on the
Turkish–Russian border, being glared at by a sentry in the Soviet
watch-tower: the only visible human being for many miles around.
There was a powerful contrast between the narrow pettiness of a
political watch-tower and the universal grandeur of a first kick . . .

DERVLA MURPHY (1931–)

Foetal Song

The vehicle gives a lurch but seems
to know its destination.
In here, antique darkness. I guess at things.
Tremors of muscles communicate
secrets to me. I am nourished.
A surge of blood pounding sweet
blossoms my gentle head.
I am perfumed wax melted of holy candles
I am ready to be fingered and shaped.

This cave unfolds to my nudge, which
seems gentle but is hard as steel
Coils of infinite steel are my secret.
Within this shadowless cave I am not confused
I think I am a fish, or a small seal.
I have an impulse to swim, but without
moving; *she* moves and I drift after . . .
I am a trout silent and gilled, a tiny seal
a slippery monster knowing all secrets.
Where is she off to now? – in high heels.
I don't like the jiggle of high heels.
On the street we hear horns, drills, feel sleeves,
feel rushes of language moving by
and every stranger has possibly
my father's face.

Now we are in bed.
Her heart breathes quiet and I drink blood.
I am juicy and sweet and coiled.
Her dreams creep upon me through nightmare slots of
    windows
I cringe from them, unready.
I don't like such pictures.
Morning . . . and the safety of the day brings us
bedroom slippers, good.

Day at home, comfort in this sac,
three months from my birthday I dream
upon songs and eerie music, angels' flutes
that tear so stern upon earthly anger
(now they are arguing again).
Jokes and unjokes, married couple,
they clutch each other in water
I feel him nudge me but it is by accident.
The darkness of their sacs must be slimy with dead tides
and hide what they knew of ponds and knotty ropes of
      lilies.
It forsakes them now, cast into the same bed.
The tide throws them relentlessly into the same bed.
While he speaks to her I suck marrow from her bones
It has a grainy white taste, a little salty.
Oxygen from her tremendous lungs tastes white too
but airy bubbly, it makes me dizzy . . . !

She speaks to him and her words do not matter.
Marrow and oxygen matter eternally. They are mine.
Sometimes she walks on concrete, my vehicle,
sometimes on gravel, on grass, on the
blank worn tides of our floors at home.
She and he, months ago, decided not to kill me.
I rise and fall now like seaweed fleshed to fish, a surprise.
I am grateful.
I am waiting for my turn.

JOYCE CAROL OATES (1938–)

from Knocked Up

JULY 27

6.15 a.m.

The itsy-bitsy spider went up the . . . went up the . . . went up the . . . something-something. I'm not sure how or why it happened this morning, but I awoke with a jolt, breathless, with this stupid nursery rhyme on my brain. Or, rather, I woke up desperate to remember the words to this stupid nursery rhyme. I can't recall what the itsy-bitsy spider did, and it's driving me nuts. I can't fall back to sleep now. Not before I figure out what the damn spider did. Will I need to know, in three months, what happened to the itsy-bitsy spider? How can I possibly be a good mother if I can't remember the itsy-bitsy spider song? How is my baby supposed to thrive when she has a mother who can't remember the words to 'The Itsy-Bitsy Spider'?

6.18 a.m.

This little piggy went to the market . . . This little piggy went to the market . . . Where did the second little piggy go? Did he go to the zoo? Did he go to the superstore? Did he go to the spa? And where did the third and fourth little piggies go? I know the last little went 'Waa waa waa' all the way home.' But what the heck did the other pigs do? I'm not going to freak. Maybe my kid won't need to know what happened to the other piggies. How important can it be to know where the second, third, and fourth piggies went? It's not exactly information that can get my kid into Harvard, is it?

REBECCA ECKLER

from A Sequence in Four Keys

I FOUGHT THE GOBLINS

Small babe, tell me
    As you sat in your mother's cave
What did you build there,
    Little baby mine?

Sir, I made the tooth
    I invented the eye
I played out hair on a comb-harp
    I thought up the sigh.

I pounded the darkness to
    Guts, Heart and Head:
America, Eurasia and Africa
    I out of chaos led.

I fought the goblins
    For the heart;
'Twas a jewel they desired.
    But I held it . . .

Small babe, tell me
    As you sit in your mother's cave
What do you build there.
    Little baby mine?

JAMES REANEY (1926–2008)

from Good Morning, Merry Sunshine

A HISTORY TOGETHER

Tonight I walked into the apartment and called hello; I heard the sounds of the television, but there was no answer. I walked into the living room, and Susan, looking tired beyond tired, was asleep on the couch. In the carriage a few feet away, Amanda slept, too.

When they awakened I could tell that this is getting to Susan. She is beginning to feel the difference – the confining difference – that the baby has brought to her world, and she can tell that, even though my world has changed, too, at least I have the discipline of my work to remind me of how things used to be.

And she feels that she and Amanda will inevitably be closer than Amanda and I. After they woke up, Amanda started hiccuping, as she often does. I said. 'Amanda, you get the hiccups all the time.'

Susan picked her up to burp her and said to her, 'He doesn't know that you used to hiccup all the time in my tummy, does he, Amanda?' Just a little reminder that they have a history together that I was never a part of.

BOB GREENE

For a Child Expected

Lovers whose lifted hands are candles in winter,
Whose gentle ways like streams in the easy summer,
Lying together
For secret setting of a child, love what they do,
Thinking they make that candle immortal, those streams forever
    flow,
And yet do better than they know.

So the first flutter of a baby felt in the womb,
Its little signal and promise of riches to come,
Is taken in its father's name,
Its life is the body of his love, like his caress,
First delicate and strange, that daily use
Makes dearer and priceless.

Our baby was to be the living sign of our joy,
Restore to each the other's lost infancy;
To a painter's pillaging eye
Poet's coiled hearing, add the heart we might earn
By the help of love; all that our passion would yield
We put to planning our child.

The world flowed in; whatever we liked we took:
For its hair, the gold curls of the November oak,
We saw on our walk;
Snowberries that make a Milky Way in the wood
For its tender hands; calm screen of the frozen flood
For our care of its childhood.

But the birth of a child is an uncontrollable glory;
Cat's cradle of hopes will hold no living baby,
Long though it lay quietly.
And when our baby stirs and struggles to be born
It compels humility: what we began
Is now its own . . .

ANNE RIDLER (1912–2001)

Happiness

An old Chinese way of describing a pregnant woman

A woman with happiness inside her

ANONYMOUS

BIRTH

Birth

Oh, fields of wonder
Out of which
Stars are born,
And moon and sun
And me as well,
Like stroke
Of lightning
In the night
Some mark
To make
Some word
To tell.

LANGSTON HUGHES (1902–67)

The Video

When Laura was born, Ceri watched.
They all gathered around Mum's bed –
Dad and the midwife and Mum's sister
and Ceri. 'Move over a bit,' Dad said –
he was trying to focus the camcorder
on Mum's legs and the baby's head.

After she had a little sister,
and Mum had gone back to being thin,
and was twice as busy, Ceri played
the video again and again.
She watched Laura come out, and then,
in reverse, she made her go back in.

FLEUR ADCOCK (1934–)

Morning Song

Love set you going like a fat gold watch,
The midwife slapped your footsoles, and your bald cry
Took its place among the elements.

Our voices echo, magnifying your arrival. New statue.
In a drafty museum, your nakedness
Shadows our safety. We stand round blankly as walls.

I'm no more your mother
Than the cloud that distils a mirror to reflect its own slow
Effacement at the wind's hand.

All night your moth-breath
Flickers among the flat pink roses. I wake to listen:
A far sea moves in my ear.

One cry, and I stumble from bed, cow-heavy and floral
In my Victorian nightgown.
Your mouth opens clean as a cat's. The window square

Whitens and swallows its dull stars. And now you try
Your handful of notes;
The clear vowels rise like balloons.

SYLVIA PLATH (1932–63)

from The American Way of Birth

TRAVAIL

The word 'travel' is derived from 'travail' denoting the pains of childbirth. There is in truth a similarity between the two conditions. Travel can be fraught with aggravating circumstances: unscheduled delays, missed connections, hanging about for hours among strangers in some remote airport, all compounded by your vivid recollections of news accounts detailing the latest spectacular plane crash. Obvious analogies will occur to those who have experienced travail.

However, the rewards soon outweigh the inconveniences – in travel, your eventual arrival at a longed-for destination; in travail, the pleasing sight and sound of a sweet newborn baby. In each case, although thoroughly exhausted, you quickly recover. A curious amnesia takes over in which all memory of the discomforts you have endured is wiped out, and your determination never, ever to do *that* again fast fades.

JESSICA MITFORD (1917–96)

Being Born Is Important

Being born is important.
You who have stood at the bedposts
and seen a mother on her high harvest day,
the day of the most golden of harvest moons for her.

You who have seen the new wet child
dried behind the ears,
swaddled in soft fresh garments,
pursing its lips and sending a groping mouth
toward the nipples where white milk is ready –

You who have seen this love's payday
of wild toil and sweet agonizing –

You know being born is important.
You know nothing else was ever so important to you.
You understand the payday of love is so old,
So involved, so traced with circles of the moon,
So cunning with the secrets of the salts of the blood –
It must be older than the moon, older than salt.

CARL SANDBURG (1878–1967)

from The Millstone

I HAD EXPECTED SO LITTLE

The midwife asked me if I would like to see the child. 'Please,' I said gratefully, and she went away and came back with my daughter wrapped up in a small grey bloodstained blanket, and with a ticket saying Stacey round her ankle. She put her in my arms and I sat there looking at her, and her great wide blue eyes looked at me with seeming recognition, and what I felt it is pointless to try to describe. Love, I suppose one might call it, and the first of my life.

I had expected so little, really. I never expect much. I had been told of the ugliness of newborn children, of their red and wrinkled faces, their waxy covering, their emaciated limbs, their hairy cheeks, their piercing cries. All I can say is that mine was beautiful and in my defence I must add that others said she was beautiful too. She was not red nor even wrinkled, but palely soft, each feature delicately reposed in its right place, and she was not bald but adorned with a thick, startling crop of black hair. One of the nurses fetched a brush and flattened it down and it covered her forehead, lying in a dense fringe that reached to her eyes. And her eyes, that seemed to see me and that looked into mine with deep gravity and charm, were a profound blue, the whites white with the gleam of alarming health. When they asked if they could have her back and put her back in her cradle for the night, I handed her over without reluctance, for the delight of holding her was too much for me. I felt as well as they that such pleasure should be regulated and rationed.

MARGARET DRABBLE (1939–)

Now That I Am Forever with Child

How the days went
while you were blooming within me
I remember each upon each –
the swelling changed planes of my body
and how you first fluttered, then jumped
and I thought it was my heart.

How the days wound down
and the turning of winter
I recall with you growing heavy
against the wind. I thought
now her hands
are formed, and her hair
has started to curl
now her teeth are done
now she sneezes.
Then the seed opened
I bore you one morning just before spring
My head rang like a fiery piston
my legs were towers between which
A new world was passing.

AUDRE LORDE (1934–92)

Labour Pains

I am sick today,
sick in my body,
eyes wide open, silent,
I lie on the bed of childbirth.

Why do I, so used to the nearness of death,
to pain and blood and screaming,
now uncontrollably tremble with dread?

A nice young doctor tried to comfort me,
and talked about the joy of giving birth.
Since I know better than he about this matter,
what good purpose can his prattle serve?

Knowledge is not reality.
Experience belongs to the past.
Let those who lack immediacy be silent.
Let observers be content to observe.

I am all alone,
totally, utterly, entirely on my own,
gnawing my lips, holding my body rigid,
waiting on inexorable fate.

There is only one truth.
I shall give birth to a child,
truth driving outward from my inwardness.
Neither good nor bad; real, no sham about it.

With the first labour pains,
suddenly the sun goes pale.
The indifferent world goes strangely calm.
I am alone.
It is alone I am.

YOSANA AKIKO (1878–1942)

Poem for a Daughter

'I think I'm going to have it,'
I said, joking between pains.
The midwife rolled competent
sleeves over corpulent milky arms.
'Dear, you never have it,
we deliver it.'
A judgement years proved true.
Certainly I've never had you

as you still have me, Caroline.
Why does a mother need a daughter
Heart's needle, hostage to fortune,
freedom's end. Yet nothing's more perfect
than that bleating, razor-shaped cry
that delivers a mother to her baby.
The bloodcord snaps that held
their sphere together. The child,
tiny and alone, creates the mother.

A woman's life is her own
until it is taken away
by a first particular cry.
Then she is not alone
but part of the premises
of everything there is:
a time, a tribe, a war.
When we belong to the world
we become what we are.

ANNE STEVENSON (1933–)

Transformation

I see you dart into the world
pearly pink like the inside of a shell
streaked with silver.

Look! Look!
I am shouting with joy, rising up
like a phoenix from my pain

With my eyes I behold you
In the flesh I behold you

So a holy man waking into death
from a life of devotion or
martyrdom in flames

might look into the shining face of god
and see at once
he had never believed.

I see you with my eyes
I see you in glory.

From a tatter of flesh I watch them work.
From a pinnacle of joy.
The placenta, purplish liver meat

sails out of my body like a whale
rubbery hands turn it inside out
hold it up to the light.

The sinewy pulsing cord.
In a haze of peace they cut and stitch
my threaded body like scarlet linen

the midwife chatting comfortably
seated at her work, the needle threaded,
the thimble, the green thread

in an out, in and out.
Then washed and trim in clean sheets
they leave us: mother father child

three folded together.
I see your sleeping face
eyelids crescent lines, lips curled translucent

in stillness like a cowrie shell
whirlpool of your hair. I see you breathe.
In a still pool the moon lies quiet.

JENI COUZYN (1942–)

Never Again an Easy Hour

Monday 9th October 1775

My wife having been seized with her pains in the night, I got up about three o'clock, and between four and five Dr Young came. He and I sat upstairs mostly till between three and four, when, after we had dined, her labour became violent. I was full of expectation, and meditated curiously on the thought that it was already certain of what sex the child was, but that l could not have the least guess on which side the probability was . . . I did not feel so much anxiety about my wife now as on former occasions, being better used to an inlying. Yet the danger was as great now as ever. I was easier from the same deception which affects a soldier who has escaped in several battles. She was very ill. Between seven and eight I went into the room. She was just delivered. I heard her say, 'God be thanked for whatever he sends.' I supposed then the child was a daughter. But she herself had not then seen it. Miss Preston said, 'Is it a daughter?' 'No,' said Mrs Forrest, the nurse-keeper, 'it's a son.' When I had seen the little man I said that I should now be so anxious that probably I should never again have an easy hour. I said to Dr Young with great seriousness, 'Doctor, Doctor, let no man set his heart upon anything in this world but land or heritable bonds; for he has no security that anything else will last as long as himself.' My anxiety subdued a flutter of joy which was in my breast. I wrote several letters to announce my son's birth. I indulged some imaginations that he might perhaps he a great man.

JAMES BOSWELL (1740–1795)

from Two Women

This then was my daughter, born in the autumn and a late fall into my life, lying purple and dented like a little bruised plum, as though she'd been lightly trodden in the grass and forgotten.

Then the Matron picked her up and she came suddenly alive, her bent legs kicking crabwise, and the first living gesture I saw was a thin wringing of the hands accompanied by a far-out Hebridean lament.

This moment of meeting seemed to be a birthtime for both of us; her first and my second life. Nothing, I knew, could ever be the same again, and I think I was reasonably shaken. I peered intently at her, looking for familiar signs, but she was as convulsed as an Aztec idol. Was this really my daughter, this purple concentration of grief, this blind and protesting dwarf?

Then they handed her to me, stiff and howling, and I held her for the first time and kissed her, and she went still and quiet as though by instinctive guile, and I was instantly enslaved by her flattery of my powers . . .

She was of course just an ordinary miracle, but was also the particular late wonder of my life. So almost every night, at first, I'd take her to bed like a book and lie close and study her. Her dark blue eyes would stare straight into mine, but off-centre, not seeing me.

Such moments could have been the best we would ever know, those midnights of mutual blindness, while I was safe from her first recognitions, and she'd stared idly through me, at the pillow, at the bedhead, at the light on the wall, and each was a shadow of indifferent importance.

Here she was then, my daughter, here, alive, the one I must possess and guard. A year before this space had been empty, not even a hope of her was in it. Now she was here, brand new, with our name upon her, and no one could call in the night to reclaim her.

LAURIE LEE (1914–97)

from Birth: A History

EMERGENCY LANDING

A woman six months pregnant went into labour on board a TWA flight that had left Kennedy Airport in New York, bound for Orlando.

'Is there a physician on board?' a member of the crew pleaded over the intercom. A flight attendant hurried to clear a row and an internist, headed to Disney World with his wife and three kids, immediately went to the side of the mother-to-be.

'My adrenaline was flowing at a hundred miles an hour,' said the man, who had only delivered one baby in his life, many years before. 'At first I thought it was false labour. But then she started bleeding. I took another look and saw the head starting to crown, and I said, "This lady is having this baby right now".'

As the plane descended for an emergency landing in the Washington area, the infant arrived with the cord wrapped around its neck. The doctor did not think the dark blue child would survive. 'I started CPR, massaged the baby's chest with two fingers, and yelled, "Breathe, baby, breathe".'

Then a husband-and-wife paramedic team – she had special infant resuscitation training – stepped in to help, calling for a straw to suction mucus from the baby's airway. A flight attendant tore a straw off a juice box stashed in her carry-on. The baby began breathing. A passenger's shoelace tied off the umbilical cord, and the child was swaddled in blue airline blankets.

'It's a boy!' the flight attendant announced. The plane erupted in cheers. All of the 213 passengers gave the mother a standing ovation as she was whisked off board. The 4-pound, 6-ounce child's middle name is Dulles, after the Virginia airport where he first touched the earth.

TINA CASSIDY

First Birth

I had thought so little, really, of *her*,
inside me, all that time, not breathing –
intelligent, maybe curious,
her eyes dosed. When the vagina opened,
slowly, from within, from the top, my eyes
rounded in shock and awe, it was like being
entered for the first time, but entered
from the inside, the child coming in
from the other world. Enormous, stately,
she was pressed through the channel, she turned, and rose,
they held her up by a very small ankle,
she dangled indigo and scarlet, and spread
her arms out in this world. Each thing
I did, then, I did for the first
time, touched the flesh of our flesh,
brought the tiny mouth to my breast,
she drew the avalanche of milk
down off the mountain, I felt as if
I was nothing, no one, I was everything to her, I was hers.

SHARON OLDS (1942–)

from Mother's Milk

NOSTALGIA FOR THE OLD WORLD

Why had they pretended to kill him when he was born? Keeping him awake for days, banging his head again and again against a closed cervix; twisting the cord around his throat and throttling him; chomping through his mother's abdomen with cold shears; clamping his head and wrenching his neck from side to side; dragging him out of his home and hitting him; shining lights in his eyes and doing experiments; taking him away from his mother while she lay on the table, half-dead. Maybe the idea was to destroy his nostalgia for the old world. First the confinement to make him hungry for space, then pretending to kill him so that he would be grateful for the space when he got it, even this loud desert, with only the bandages of his mother's arms to wrap around him, never the whole thing again, the whole warm thing all around him, being everything.

The curtains were breathing light into their hospital room. Swelling from the hot afternoon, and then flopping back against the French windows, easing the glare outside.

Someone opened the door and the curtains leapt up and rippled their edges; loose paper rustled, the room whitened, and the shudder of the roadworks grew a little louder. Then the door clunked and the curtains sighed and the room dimmed . . .

The nurse looked at Robert and he locked on to her blue eyes in the heaving dimness.

'He's very alert. He's really checking me out.'

EDWARD ST AUBYN (1960–)

Woman to Child

You who were darkness warmed my flesh
where out of darkness rose the seed.
Then all a world I made in me;
all the world you hear and see
hung upon my dreaming blood.

There moved the multitudinous stars,
and coloured birds and fishes moved.
There swarm the sliding continents.
All time lay rolled in me, and sense,
and love that knew not its beloved.

O node and focus of the world;
I hold you deep within that well
you shall escape and not escape –
that mirrors still your sleeping shape;
that nurtures still your crescent cell.

I wither and you break from me;
yet though you dance in living light
I am the earth, I am the root,
I am the stem that fed the fruit,
the link that joins you to the night.

JUDITH WRIGHT (1915–2000)

from Flush

THE BABY AND THE DOG

One day early in March Mrs Browning did not appear in the sitting-room at all. Other people came in and out; Mr Browning and Wilson came in and out; and they came in and out so distractedly that Flush hid himself under the sofa. People were trampling up and down stairs, running and calling in low whispers and muted unfamiliar voices. They were moving upstairs in the bedroom. He crept further and further under the shadow of the sofa. He knew in every fibre of his body that some change was taking place – some awful event was happening . . .

At last Wilson, looking very flushed and untidy but triumphant, took him in her arms and carried him upstairs. They entered the bedroom. There was a faint bleating in the shadowed room – something waved on the pillow. It was a live animal. Independently of them all, without the street door being opened, out of herself in the room, alone, Mrs Browning had become two people. The horrid thing waved and mewed by her side. Torn with rage and jealousy and some deep disgust that he could not hide, Flush struggled himself free and rushed downstairs. Wilson and Mrs Browning called him back; they tempted him with caresses; they offered him titbits; but it was useless. He cowered away from the disgusting sight, the repulsive presence, wherever there was a shadowy sofa or a dark corner. '. . . for a whole fortnight he fell into deep melancholy and was proof against all attentions lavished on him' – so Mrs Browning, in the midst of all her other distractions, was forced to notice. And when we take, as we must, human minutes and hours and drop them into a dog's mind and see how the minutes swell into hours and the hours into days, we shall not exaggerate if we conclude that Flush's 'deep melancholy' lasted six full months by the human clock. Many men and women have forgotten their hates and their loves in less.

VIRGINIA WOOLF (1882–1941)

Baby Song

From the private ease of Mother's womb
I fall into the lighted room.

Why don't they simply put me back
Where it is warm and wet and black?

But one thing follows on another.
Things were different inside Mother.

Padded and jolly I would ride
The perfect comfort of her inside.

They tuck me in a rustling bed
– I lie there, raging, small, and red.

I may sleep soon. I may forget.
But I won't forget that I regret.

A rain of blood poured round her womb.
But all time roars outside this room.

THOM GUNN (1929–2004)

from Anna Karenina

NEW JOY

Like a flame above a lamp, flickered in Mary Vlasevna's skilful hands the life of a human being who had never before existed: a human being who, with the same right and the same importance to himself, would live and would procreate others like himself.

'Alive! Alive! And a boy! Don't be anxious,' Levin heard Mary Vlasevna say, as she slapped the baby's back with a shaking hand.

'Mama, is it true?' asked Kitty.

The Princess could only sob in reply.

And amid the silence, as a positive answer to the mother's question, a voice quite unlike all the restrained voices that had been speaking in the room made itself heard. It was a bold, insolent voice that had no consideration for anything, it was the cry of the new human being who had so incomprehensibly appeared from some unknown realm.

Before that, if Levin had been told that Kitty was dead, and that he had died with her, that they had angel children, and that God was there present with them – he would not have been astonished. But now, having returned to the world of actuality, he had to make great efforts to understand that she was alive and well, and that the creature that was yelling so desperately was his son. Kitty was alive, her sufferings were over, and he was full of unspeakable bliss. This he comprehended, and it rendered him entirely happy. But the child? When and why had he come? Who was he? . . . He could not at all accustom himself to the idea. It seemed something superfluous, something overflowing, and for a long time he was unable to get used to it.

LEO TOLSTOY (1828–1910)

The Birthnight

Dearest, it was a night
That in its darkness rocked Orion's stars;
A sighing wind ran faintly white
Along the willows, and the cedar boughs
Laid their wide hands in stealthy peace across
The starry silence of their antique moss:
No sound save rushing air
Cold, yet all sweet with Spring,
And in thy mother's arms, couched weeping there,
    Thou, lovely thing.

WALTER DE LA MARE (1873–1956)

NAMINGS AND BLESSINGS

Choosing a Name

I have got a new-born sister;
I was nigh the first that kissed her.
When the nursing woman brought her
To papa, his infant daughter,
How papa's dear eye did glisten!
She will shortly be to christen:
And papa has made the offer,
I shall have the naming of her.

Now I wonder what would please her,
Charlotte, Julia, or Louisa.
Ann and Mary, they're too common;
Joan's too formal for a woman;
Jane's a prettier name beside;
But we had a Jane that died.
They would say, if 'twas Rebecca,
That she was a little Quaker.
Edith's pretty, but that looks
Better in old English books;
Ellen's left off long ago;
Blanche is out of fashion now.
None that I have named as yet
Are so good as Margaret.
Emily is neat and fine.
What do you think of Caroline?
How I'm puzzled and perplexed
What to choose or think of next!
I am in a little fever.
Lest the name that I shall give her
Should disgrace her or defame her,
I will leave papa to name her.

CHARLES and MARY LAMB
(1775–1834) and (1764–1847)

The Angel That Presided O'er My Birth

The Angel that presided o'er my birth
Said, 'Little creature, form'd of Joy & Mirth,
'Go love without the help of any Thing on Earth.'

WILLIAM BLAKE (1757–1827)

from For a Christening

INVOCATION

Blessing, sleep and grow taller in sleeping.
Lie ever in kind keeping.
Infants curl in a cowrie of peace
And should lie lazy. After this ease,
When the soul out of its safe shell goes,
Stretched as you stretch those knees and toes,
What should I wish you? Intelligence first,
In a credulous age by instruction cursed.
Take from us both what immunity
We have from the germ of the printed lie.
Your father's calm temper I wish you, and
The shaping of power of his confident hand.
Much, too, that is different and your own;
And may we learn to leave you alone.
For your part, forgive us the pain of living,
Grow in that harsh sun great-hearted and loving.
Sleep, little honey, then; sleep while the powers
Of the Nine Bright Shiners and the Seven Stars
Harmless, encircle: the natural world
Lifegiving, neutral, unless despoiled
By our greed or scorn. And wherever you sleep –
My arms outgrown – or waking weep,
Life is your lot: you lie in God's hand,
In his terrible mercy, world without end.

ANNE RIDLER (1912–2001)

They Might Not Need Me – Yet They Might

They might not need me – yet they might
I'll let my heart be just in sight –
A smile so small as mine might be
Precisely their necessity.

EMILY DICKINSON (1830–86)

'Like a Fish Out of God's Hand'

Like a fish out of God's hand
she fell and looked for her element,

the prints of her fingers
felt through the scales,

the warmth of her hand came up
like a gulf stream

and she swam,
over the galaxies, over the star trails,

over the moon and the borders of cloud
into my hand,

and she beat there like a fish not caught,
knowing everything water,

and I thought, how can I live up to it,
how can I catch from the hand of God

this fish, and while I was thinking
she slipped out

and made her own way into sea,
even without any water.

DESMOND GRAHAM (1940–)

from De Rerum Natura, Book 5

THE CHILD IS LIKE A SAILOR CAST UP BY THE SEA

The child is like a sailor cast up by the sea,
Lying naked on the shore, unable to speak,
Helpless, when first it comes to the light of day,
Shed from the womb through all the pains of labour,
And fills the place with cries as well it might,
Having a life of so many ills before it.
Yet flocks and herds, to say nothing of wild beasts,
Don't need a rattle or anything of that kind
Nor even a nurse to feed them with baby-talk:
Nor do they need sets of clothes for summer and winter.
One may add that they don't need weapons or high walls
To keep them safe, they find themselves perfectly happy
Walking around in a world which produces plenty.

LUCRETIUS (*c.*94 BC–*c.*55)

I Am So Small

I am so small
I can barely be seen.
How can this great
Love be inside me?
Look at your eyes.
They are small,
But they see
Enormous things.

RUMI (1207–73)

from The Bloomsbury Christening

HUM OF ADMIRATION

'Now, uncle,' said Mr Kitterbell, lifting that part of the mantle which covered the infant's face, with an air of great triumph, '*who* do you think he's like?'

'He! He! Yes, who?' said Mrs K., putting her arm through her husband's, and looking up into Dump's face with an expression of as much interest as she was capable of displaying.

'Good God, how small he is!' cried the amiable uncle, starting back with well-feigned surprise; '*remarkably* small indeed.'

'Do you think so?' inquired poor little Kitterbell, rather alarmed. 'He's a monster to what he was – ain't he, nurse?'

'He's a dear,' said the nurse, squeezing the child . . .

A general hum of admiration interrupted the conversation . . . An universal rush of the young ladies immediately took place. (Girls are always *so* fond of babies in company.)

'Oh, you dear!' said one.

'How sweet!' cried another, in a low tone of the most enthusiastic admiration.

'Heavenly!' added a third.

'Oh, what dear little arms!' said a fourth . . .

'Did you ever?' – said a little coquette with a large bustle, who looked like a French lithograph, appealing to a gentleman in three waistcoats – 'did you ever?'

'Never in my life,' returned her admirer, pulling up his collar.

'Oh! *do* let me take it, nurse,' cried another young lady. 'The love!'

'Can it open its eyes, nurse?' inquired another, affecting the utmost innocence. – Suffice it to say that the single ladies unanimously voted him an angel, and that the married ones, *nem.con.*, agreed that he was decidedly the finest baby they had ever beheld – except their own . . .

CHARLES DICKENS (1812–70)

Infant Joy

'I have no name:
'I am but two days old.'
What shall I call thee?
'I happy am,
'Joy is my name.'
Sweet joy befall thee!

Pretty joy!
Sweet joy but two days old,
Sweet joy I call thee:
Thou dost smile,
I sing the while,
Sweet joy befall thee!

Infant Sorrow

My mother groan'd, my father wept,
Into the dangerous world I leapt;
Helpless, naked, piping loud,
Like a fiend hid in a cloud.

Struggling in my father's hands,
Striving against my swadling bands,
Bound and weary, I thought best
To sulk upon my mother's breast.

WILLIAM BLAKE (1757–1827)

Mighty Like a Rose

Sweetest little feller,
Everybody knows;
Don't know what to call him,
But he's mighty like a rose.

Looking at his Mammy
With eyes so shiny blue,
Make you think that heaven
Is coming close to you.

FRANK L. STANTON (1857–1927)

The Spirit is too Blunt an Instrument

The spirit is too blunt an instrument
to have made this baby.
Nothing so unskilful as human passions
could have managed the intricate
exacting particulars: the tiny
blind bones with their manipulating tendons,
the knee and the knucklebones, the resilient
fine meshings of ganglia and vertebrae
in the chain of the difficult spine.

Observe the distinct eyelashes and sharp crescent
fingernails, the shell-like complexity
of the ear with its firm involutions
concentric in miniature to the minute
ossicles. Imagine the
infinitesimal capillaries, the flawless connections
of the lungs, the invisible neural filaments
through which the completed body
already answers to the brain.

Then name any passion or sentiment
possessed of the simplest accuracy.
No. No desire or affection could have done
with practice what habit
has done perfectly, indifferently,
through the body's ignorant precision.
It is left to the vagaries of the mind to invent
love and despair and anxiety
and their pain.

ANNE STEVENSON (1933–)

Fain Would I Dive

Fain would I dive to find my infant self
In the unfathom'd ocean of the past:
I can but find a sun-burnt prattling elf,
A forward urchin of four years at least.

The prettiest speech – 'tis in my mind engrain'd –
That first awaked me from my babyhood,
Twas a grave saw affectionately feign'd –
'We'll love you little master, – if you're good.'

Sweet babe thou art not yet or good or bad,
Yet God is round thee, in thee, and above thee;
We love, because we love thee, little lad,
And pray thou may'st be good – because we love thee.

HARTLEY COLERIDGE (1796–1849)

from The Baby

Where did you come from, baby dear?
Out of the everywhere into the here.

Where did you get your eyes so blue?
Out of the sky as I came through.

What makes the light in them sparkle and spin?
Some of the starry spikes left in.

Where did you get that little tear?
I found it waiting when I got here.

What makes your forehead so smooth and high?
A soft hand stroked it as I went by.

What makes your cheek like a warm white rose?
Something better than any one knows.

GEORGE MACDONALD (1824–1905)

from The Salutation

From dust I rise,
And out of nothing now awake,
These brighter regions which salute mine eyes,
A gift from God I take.
The earth, the seas, the light, the day, the skies,
The sun and stars are mine; if those I prize . . .

A stranger here
Strange things doth meet, strange glories see;
Strange treasures lodg'd in this fair world appear;
Strange all, and new to me.
But that they mine should be, who nothing was,
That strangest is of all, yet brought to pass.

THOMAS TRAHERNE (*c.*1637–74)

Whatsoever Things Are True

Whatsoever things are true,
whatsoever things are honest,
whatsoever things are just,
whatsoever things are pure,
whatsoever things are lovely,
whatsoever things are of good report:
if there be any virtue,
and if there be any praise,
think on these things.

PHILIPPIANS 4:8

Morning Has Broken

Morning has broken
Like the first morning,
Blackbird has spoken
Like the first bird.
Praise for the singing,
Praise for the morning,
Praise for them, springing
Fresh from the Word!

Sweet the rain's new fall
Sunlit from heaven,
Like the first dewfall
On the first grass.
Praise for the sweetness
Of the wet garden,
Sprung in completeness
Where His feet pass.

Mine is the sunlight;
Mine is the morning.
Born of the one light
Eden saw play!
Praise with elation,
Praise every morning,
God's re-creation
Of the new day!

ELEANOR FARJEON (1881–1965)

A Little Child

And he came to Capernaum: and being in the house he asked them, What was it that ye disputed among yourselves by the way?

But they held their peace: for by the way they had disputed among themselves, who who should be the greatest.

And he sat down, and called the twelve, and saith unto them,

If any man desire to be first, the same shall be last of all, and servant of all.

And he took a child, and set him in the midst of them: and when he had taken him in his arms, he said unto them, Whosoever shall receive one of such children in my name, receiveth me: and whosoever shall receive me, receiveth not me, but him that sent me.

St Mark 9: 33–7

To Such as These

And they brought young children to him, that he should touch them: and the disciples rebuked those that brought them. But when Jesus saw it, he was much displeased, and said unto them, Suffer the little children to come unto me, and forbid them not: for of such is the kingdom of God.

Verily I say unto you, Whosoever shall not receive the kingdom of God as a little child, he shall not enter therein.

And he took them up in his arms, put his hands upon them, and blessed them.

St Mark 10: 13–16

Away in a Manger

Away in a manger, no crib for a bed,
The little Lord Jesus laid down His sweet head;
The stars in the bright sky looked down where He lay
The little Lord Jesus, asleep on the hay.

The cattle are lowing, the baby awakes,
But little Lord Jesus, no crying He makes.
I love Thee, Lord Jesus! Look down from the sky,
And stay by my side until morning is nigh.

Be near me, Lord Jesus: I ask Thee to stay
Close by me for ever, and love me, I pray;
Bless all the dear children in Thy tender care,
And fit us for heaven to live with Thee there.

ANONYMOUS

from The Prophet

THE HOUSE OF TOMORROW

And a woman who held a babe against her bosom said, Speak to us
of Children.
And he said:
Your children are not your children.
They are the sons and daughters of Life's longing for itself.
They come through you but not from you,
And though they are with you yet they belong not to you.

You may give them your love but not your thoughts,
For they have their own thoughts.
You may house their bodies but not their souls,
For their souls dwell in the house of tomorrow, which you cannot
visit, not even in your dreams.
You may strive to be like them, but seek not to make them like
you.
For life goes not backward nor tarries with yesterday.

You are the bows from which your children as living arrows are
sent forth.
The Archer sees the mark upon the path of infinite, and He bends
you with His might that arrows may go swift and far.
Let your bending in the Archer's hand be for gladness;
For even as He loves the arrow that flies, so He loves also the bow
that is stable.

KAHLIL GIBRAN (1883–1931)

A Time to Be Born

To every thing there is a season, and a time to every purpose under the heaven:

a time to be born, and a time to die;

a time to plant, and a time to pluck up that which is planted;

a time to kill, and a time to heal;

a time to break down, and a time to build up;

a time to weep, and a time to laugh;

a time to mourn, and a time to dance;

a time to cast away stones, and a time to gather stones together;

a time to embrace, and a time to refrain from embracing;

a time to get, and a time to lose;

a time to keep, and a time to cast away;

a time to rend, and a time to sew;

a time to keep silence, and a time to speak;

a time to love, and a time to hate;

a time of war, and a time of peace.

ECCLESIASTES 3: 1–8

Cradle Song

Erce . . . Erce . . . Erce
Primigravida

curled like a hoop in sleep
unearthly of manufacture,
tissue of blossom and clay
bone the extract of air
fountain of nature.

softly knitted by kisses,
added to stitch by stitch,
by sleep of the dying heart,
by water and wool and air,
gather a fabric rich.

earth contracted to earth
in ten toes: the cardinals.
in ten fingers: the bishops.
ears by two, eyes by two,
watch the mirror watching you,

and now hush

the nightwalkers bringing peace,
seven the badges of grace
five the straw caps of talent,
one the scarf of desire, go
mimic your mother's lovely face.

LAWRENCE DURRELL (1912–90)

from Gilead

You feel an obligation to a child when you have seen it and held it. Any human face is a claim on you, because you can't help but understand the singularity of it, the courage and loneliness of it.

MARILYNNE ROBINSON (1947–)

MOTHER LOVE

To My Daughter

I have a child; so fair
As golden flowers is she,
My Cleïs, all my care.
I'd not give her away
For Lydia's wide sway
Nor lands men long to see.

SAPPHO (600 BC)

Hush, Little Baby, Don't Say a Word

Hush, little baby, don't say a word,
Mama's gonna buy you a mockingbird.

If that mockingbird don't sing,
Mama's gonna buy you a diamond ring.

If that diamond ring is brass,
Mama's gonna buy you a looking glass.

If that looking glass gets broke,
Mama's gonna buy you a billy-goat.

If that billy-goat won't pull,
Mama's gonna buy you a cart and bull.

If that card and bull turns over,
Mama's gonna buy you a dog named Rover.

If that dog named Rover won't bark,
Mama's gonna buy you a horse and cart.

If that horse and cart falls down,
You'll still be the sweetest little baby in town.

TRADITIONAL

Latching On

Your head's cloaked in my bath-robe
as you jut my breast, frantic to dock.
In the gaunt light of late night tv
you beat me with your fists and shriek
for milk.
          I strip us both, lie giant
on the bed and set you on my stomach
where you clamber, eyes bigger
and exhausted with knowledge.
You root my belly, ribs, even
the clavicle's hard edge,
but when you find a nipple
you take the breast in adult,
outstretched hands, your lower lip
splays, toothless gums sink
into me, and the rhythmic suck
draws us flush. Then a rusty
connection from nipple to uterus
tautens, and my innards shirr
on an ancient wire.
          And the way
you look at me, as the drink gathers
its gulping momentum, has a religious
stillness. It sees, soberly, past all
my fragile edges. Like a lover's eyes.
Or rather, a lover's like yours.

SALLY READ (1971–)

Human Affection

Mother, I love you so.
Said the child, I love you more than I know.
She laid her head on her mother's arm,
And the love between them kept them warm.

STEVIE SMITH (1902–71)

from Separation

THE SECRET

Let me stop a moment to introduce a little known character, the chief character in so many real-life scenarios, although severely neglected in literature and plays. Let me introduce THE BABY, at present fast asleep in her cot, eyes fluttering to the universal tune of Brahm's lullaby, looking mild and peaceful. THE BABY is a figure of enormous consequence, never to be underestimated. Watch a baby of a few weeks kick its legs. Oh – the power of that soft skin and appealing blue eyes. Lovers – beware of babies. The baby wants the mother all to itself. It doesn't want the father with his bristly chin. Go away father. Go back to your work. I shall wake my mother at night. I shall stare searchingly into her eyes. I will need her so much she will forget all about you. And you will be left alone in your bed. She will cease to buy clothes for herself. She will buy them only for me. I will suck at her breasts. I restore her and destroy her. She will wash the creases of my fat thighs. She will long for me to sleep and when I sleep she will long for me to wake. She is in love, you see. Shhh . . . it's the secret women never tell. You were just the booby trap nature set up to send her hurtling into my arms. All the make-up she put on and the pounding music you listened to, and the hot kisses you shared, it all leads only to me, the beginning and the end of things, a new age-old bald person, a Buddha giving meaning and taking it all away.

SALLY EMERSON

Her First Week

She was so small I would scan the crib a half-second
to find her, face-down in a corner, limp
as something gently flung down, or fallen
from some sky an inch above the mattress. I would
tuck her arm along her side
and slowly turn her over. She would tumble
over part by part, like a load
of damp laundry in the dryer, I'd slip
a hand in, under her neck,
slide the other under her back,
and evenly lift her up. Her little bottom
sat in my palm, her chest contained
the puckered, moire sacs, and her neck –
I was afraid of her neck, once I almost
thought I heard it quietly snap,
I looked at her and she swivelled her slate
eyes and looked at me. It was in
my care, the creature of her spine, like the first
chordate, as if, history
of the vertebrate had been placed in my hands.
Every time I checked, she was still
with us – someday, there would be a human
race. I could not see it in her eves,
but when I fed her, gathered her
like a loose bouquet to my side and offered
the breast, greyish-white, and struck with
minuscule scars like creeks in sunlight, I
felt she was serious, I believed she was willing to stay.

SHARON OLDS (1942–)

Fetching the Moon

How lovely you are, you seem to have no flaws.
What shall I bring which is as flawless?
    Hush, sleep.
Let me go and fetch the moon,
The flawless moon and the stars.
    Hush, sleep.

How lovely you are, you seem to have no flaws.
Every part of you is so dear.
    Hush, sleep.
But you do have one flaw!
You are not sleepy, you stay awake.
    Hush, sleep.

TRADITIONAL, ARMENIAN

Mine

Someone would like to have you for her child
But you are mine.
Someone would like to rear you on a costly mat
But you are mine.
Someone would like to place you on a camel blanket
But you are mine.
I have you to rear on a torn old mat.
Someone would like to have you as her child
But you are mine.

AKAN PEOPLE, AFRICA

Mammy, Mammy Told Me-o

Mammy, mammy told me-o.
I'm the sweetest little baby in the country-o.
I looked in the glass and found it so,
Just as mammy told me-o.

TRADITIONAL

from Love Forty

SMASHING THE SUN

I wasn't really prepared for mother love. I'd read so many accounts of maternal indifference: the depression that can set in; the difficulty in relating to the new baby. Knowing how unmaternal I had always been, I'd assumed I'd go that way. My first glimpse of my daughter had been a strange surprise: almost embarrassing, as meeting any stranger is, for the first few moments, embarrassing. I could see very well that she was not what you'd call beautiful. All the same, when she cried her deep soulful cry, I was filled not merely with panic but with passion. I loved her even more for not being beautiful.

But was she comfortable? Were those sunbeams perhaps a little too strong? Did they cause her a moment's inconvenience? I would smash the sun to smithereens if they did. It would be the work of a moment: nothing easier. I would weep tears of anguish the while. There seemed to be lots of anguish about. I only had to imagine her suffering anything at the hands of anybody and I sprouted claws and fangs. I would tear her assailants limb from limb. Motherhood seemed to have turned me, overnight, into a sabre-toothed tiger.

SUE LIMB (1946–)

A Cossack Mother's Song to Her Baby

Sleep, my baby, sleep, my pretty,
Bai-ush-ki bayu,
While the moon is shining clearly
From above on you,
I will tell you many stories
And will sing to you!
Close your eyes and keep on dreaming,
Bai-ush-ki bayu!

Over stones the streaming Terek
Splashes muddy waves.
Wicked Tchetchen with his dagger
Creeps along the shore.
But your father, an old warrior,
He was stabbed in war;
Sleep my baby, do not worry,
Bai-ush-ki bayu!

You will learn yourself when ready –
Of the warrior's life;
Boldly you will set your stirrup
And will take your gun.
And your little soldier's saddle
I with silks will sew.
Sleep, my own dear child, my baby,
Bai-ush-ki bayu!

Like a hero in appearance,
But a Cossack in your heart,
I shall come to see you leaving
And you'll wave farewell.
Oh, what bitter tears of sorrow
I will shed that night!
Sleep my angel, softly, sweetly,
Bai-ush-ki bayu!

TRADITIONAL

Any Babe

The world has no such flowers in any land
And no such pearl in any gulf the sea,
As any babe on any mother's knee.

ALGERNON CHARLES SWINBURNE (1837–1909)

Dawn

Of your hand I could say this
a bird poised mid-air in flight
as delicate and smooth.

Of your mouth
a foxglove in its taking
without edges or hurt.

This of your ear
a tiny sea-horse, immortal
sporting in white waves

and of your eye
a place where no one could hide
nothing lurk.

Of your cupped flesh
smooth in my palm
an agate on the sea-shore

of your back and belly
that they command kisses.
And of your feet I would say

they are inquisitive and gay
as squirrels or birds
and so return to your hand

and begin my voyage
around your loveliness
again and yet again

as in my arms you lie sleeping.

JENI COUZYN (1942–)

This Crying Thing

A few nights ago, when I was alone in the house with him, he reduced me to sobs of exhausted despair because he kept dragging me from my bed with impossible demands for sweets, television and bottles of milk. I am sorry to say that in the end we were in competition, to see who could howl the loudest.

'Stop this game!' he rapped out furiously.

'What bloody game?'

'This crying thing – stop it at once!'

Believe me, I would gladly stop this crying thing, if only I could stop taking everything so personally. Never mind the evening news, or the novels of Dostoevsky; I get to the last page of Shirley Hughes's *Lucy and Tom's Christmas*, and cannot utter the words, 'Happy Christmas Lucy and Tom, happy Christmas everyone!' without my voice suddenly shooting up an octave, as if I'd swallowed a helium balloon. Tears rush to my eyes whenever Postman Pat performs one of his many acts of kindness. I bleed for Eeyore, on his forgotten birthday.

Having a baby buggers up your emotions. 'A sword shall pierce your heart,' Simeon told Mary, as she carried the infant Jesus into the temple. He might have added that a sword shall pierce the heart of every mother in the world.

KATE SAUNDERS

from Disobedience

James James
Morrison Morrison
Weatherby George Dupree
Took great
Care of his Mother
Though he was only three . . .

A. A. Milne (1882–1956)

One or the Other

To be a mother I must leave the telephone unanswered, work undone, arrangements unmet. To be myself I must let the baby cry, must forestall her hunger or leave her for evenings out, must forget her in order to think about other things. To succeed in being one means to fail at being the other.

RACHEL CUSK (1967–)

Daystar

She wanted a little room for thinking:
but she saw diapers steaming on the line,
a doll slumped behind the door.

So she lugged a chair behind the garage
to sit out the children's naps.

Sometimes there were things to watch –
the pinched armor of a vanished cricket,
a floating maple leaf. Other days
she stared until she was assured
when she closed her eyes
she'd see only her own vivid blood.

She had an hour, at best, before Liza appeared
pouting from the top of the stairs.
And just *what* was mother doing
out back with the field mice? Why,

building a palace. Later
that night when Thomas rolled over and
lurched into her, she would open her eyes
and think of the place that was hers
for an hour – where
she was nothing,
pure nothing, in the middle of the day.

RITA DOVE (1952–)

Sweet Torment

Every time I knelt at the altar-rail in church, I would watch the priest blessing the heads of the babies, and pray for a child of my own. My prayer was heard, and I was admitted to the most intense joy on this earth. But I was not prepared for the sorrow of it all.

I have shed tears over my real boy, every single day of his life. Before I had him, I liked to think of myself as a temperate and well-ordered sort of person. Actually, I turn out to be a demented maenad, who screams and hurls plates. I am a soggy, boggy Niobe; a battered victim utterly beset and cowed by testosterone.

Our relationship neatly encapsulates the ancient and world-wide power struggle between men and women. I love Felix to distraction. I am sure the love would be exactly the same temperature if I had been blessed with a daughter instead, but doubt that I would be enslaved in quite the same way. It is the stormiest love affair of my life. If this was a real love affair, my friends would beg me to leave him.

He beats me like a gong, then melts me with his remorse afterwards . . .

Perhaps I should date my depression from the bodily upheaval of pregnancy. We had trundled along fairly quietly together for 32 years, my body and I. Like an unexciting but reliable old car – a Volvo, say – it had given me hardly a lick of trouble in all that time. Its weight neither rose nor fell. Its skin was serviceable and unlined.

And then I got pregnant. I gave up smoking, and became hugely fat. In the final month, I had severe oedema, and had to waddle to the jeweller's to have my wedding ring sawn off my finger. Looking back, this seems highly symbolic. My body had chosen Felix, and elected to slough off his father. It had become a grow-bag, for the protection and nurture of someone far more important.

The thing inside was also more important than me. I was no longer the heroine of my own life.

KATE SAUNDERS

from A Life's Work

A VALEDICTION TO SLEEP

I remember the night sleep left me. It happened in hospital. I had suspected nothing. Several hours earlier I had had a baby; people had come and gone, flowers had been brought. Darkness fell. Presently it was half past ten or so, time to go to sleep. I wrapped the baby up in blankets like a new purchase, a present that I would unwrap and look at again in the morning. I slept. When I woke again some time later, it was to realise with real surprise that the terrible, persistent wailing racketing through the ward was 'me', as people now say of their mobile phones. My new purchase had gone off in the dead of night like some alarm I didn't know how to disconnect . . .

The baby continued to wake three or four times each night, and each time I was ready for her, trained and vigilant as a soldier. I no longer, it seemed, slept at all in the intervals, but merely rested silently like some legendary figure, itinerant, doughty and far from home. The reservoir of sleep I had accumulated through my life had run dry. I was living off air and adrenalin. Mercury ran through my veins. I wondered if this parched and dogged wraithe long since severed from its human past was in fact that dark stranger who walks the world of childhood wreathed in mystery: a parent.

RACHEL CUSK (1967–)

The Waiting

You quietened when they held your face to mine,
as though you'd entered a house, out of the wind.
Your scrunched eyes waxed to black,
did the telescopic slide as you took me in.
My arms were dead so it was left to them
to rub your cheek to mine, and back again.
Then they took you away to scream.
Two hours of waiting. They tugged up the skin
of my legs to mend the rent you made;

wheeled me to a room on my own, my thoughts
lobbed off by morphine, my body half-gone.
I want you to know I was an amnesiac
in those hours. My old life was yesterday's
clothes: ill-fitting, redundant with blood.
My sappy nerves revved under the weight
of dead legs, but there was no beginning.
I waited without expectation or any way out,
as though I waited for my own name.

SALLY READ (1971–)

A Child's Sleep

I stood at the edge of my child's sleep
hearing her breathe:
although I could not enter there.
I could not leave.

Her sleep was a small wood,
perfumed with flowers;
dark, peaceful, sacred,
acred in hours.

And she was the spirit that lives
in the heart of such woods:
without time, without history,
wordlessly good.

I spoke her name, a pebble dropped
in the still night,
and saw her stir, both open palms
cupping their soft light:

then went to the window. The greater dark
outside the room
gazed back, maternal, wise,
with its face of moon.

CAROL ANN DUFFY (1955–)

Men Scale Other Heights

There is nothing on earth like
the moment of seeing one's first baby.
Men scale other heights,
but there is no height like
this simple one,
occurring continuously throughout
all the ages in musty bedrooms,
in palaces, in caves and desert places.
I looked at this rolled-up bundle . . .
and knew again I had not
created her. She was herself
apart from me.
She had her own life to lead,
her own destiny to accomplish;
she just came past me
to this earth.

KATHERINE TREVELYAN

Mother and Child

To me, motherhood is the most complete relationship of all. I'm absolutely baffled by the way every book is about the man-woman relationship. It's fine, it's lovely, it makes for a lot of delight and companionship. But I think a mother and child is of infinitely more significance, infinitely more interesting than romantic love. To me, it's the whole point and purpose of life . . . Of course there's that awful thing of having to love them and then let them go. It's terribly hard. It's not that you want to keep them, it's that you want to know that they are going to be *safe*. For ever.

ALICE THOMAS ELLIS (1932–2005)

from The First Year

As monks whose time is told by bells
Out of the strict hours see eternity,
I have watched your eternity, your world without
    beginning
These five months by the moon;

These days by the clock with their ritual repetitions,
Votive milk and early rising,
Plains of peace and fainting terrors,
And their meaning out of time.

For between one feed and another,
Your sleep's forgetting, your calms of waking
Have freed me to eternity
Like the sky through a little window-frame.

E. J. SCOVELL

from Blackberry Winter: My Earlier Years

BUT THE BABY SMILES SO MUCH

I remember the flash of insight I had in 1940 as I sat talking to a small delegation that had come to ask me to address a women's congress. I had my baby on my lap, and as we talked I recalled my psychology professor's explanation of why women are less productive than men. He had referred to a letter written by Harriet Beecher Stowe in which she said that she had in mind to write a novel about slavery, but the baby cried so much. It suddenly occurred to me that it would have been much more plausible if she had said 'but the baby smiles so much'. It is not that women have less impulse than men to be creative and productive. But through the ages having children, for women who wanted children, has been so satisfying that it has taken some special circumstance – spinsterhood, barrenness, or widowhood – to let women give their whole minds to other work.

MARGARET MEAD (1901–78)

Some Days, Mother

Some days, mother
when my thoughts are a tangle I cannot untie
when meanings are lost and I cannot say why
when the daily drudging is exhausting not fulfilling
when a hollow inside says I'm existing not living
Those days, mother
when life is a circle that keeps me spinning not moving

Who else in the world could I tell of the pain?
Who else in the world would understand the hurt?
Who else in the world would I simply know is sharing?
Who else in the world could so love me in weakness?
Who else, mother? who else?

Some days, mother
when the coming of morning is an intrusion I fear
when the falling of night fuels thoughts of despair
when prayer for some deeper believing
is a passion I cannot express
when the tolling of time seems so slow
and so pointless

Who else in the world could I tell of the hurt?
Who else in the world wouldn't think me insane?
Who else in the world could love me
just for the sake of loving?
Who else, mother? Who else?

Some days, mother
when I can find no meaning
even in your existence
when we quarrel and argue
and I really wish I never knew you
when I listen and look at you

and hope I'm not seeing my future
when some other searching
has fuelled rejection

Who else in the world
would just love me again without question?
Who else holds this feeling
that nothing I do can erase?
Who else is simply always there for my story?
Who else, mother? Who else?

Some days, mother,
when I go searching for this kind of loving you're giving
when I go giving this kind of loving you're teaching
It's like trying to hold
the rainbow that drinks in the river
It's like trying to hug
the moonlight that sits on the doorstep
It's like spinning around in circles
and challenging the sky to come falling

So mother, tell me
Who else knows the secret of this deeper loving?
Who else shares the miracle of such tender caring?
Who else is there that knows
of this unstinting supporting?
Who else, mother?
Who else?

MERLE COLLINS (1950–)

Mother and Daughter

She will not have it that my day wanes low,
Poor of the fire its drooping sun denies,
That on my brow the thin lines write goodbyes
Which soon may be read plain for all to know,
Telling that I have done with youth's brave show;
Alas! and done with youth in hearts and eyes,
With wonder and with far expectancies,
Save but to say 'I knew such long ago.'

She will not have it. Loverlike to me,
She with her happy gaze finds all that's best,
She sees this fair and that unfretted still,
And her own sunshine over all the rest;
So she half keeps me as she'd have me be,
And I forget to age, through her sweet will.

AUGUSTA WEBSTER (1837–94)

Blue Muslin

My sole consolation when I went
upstairs for the night was that
Mamma would come in and kiss
me after I was in bed. But this
good night lasted for so short a
time, she went down again so
soon, that the moment in which
I heard her climb the stairs, and
then caught the sound of her
garden dress of blue muslin, from
which hung little tassels of
plaited straw, rustling along the
double-doored corridor, was for
me a moment of the utmost pain;
for it heralded the moment
which was bound to follow it,
when she would have left me and
gone downstairs again . . .

MARCEL PROUST (1871–1922)

Her Laugh

Certainly there she was, in the very centre of that great Cathedral space which was childhood; there she was from the very first. My first memory is of her lap; the scratch of some beads on her dress comes back to me as I pressed my cheek against it. Then I see her in her white dressing gown on the balcony; and the passion flower with the purple star on its petals. Her voice is still faintly in my ears – decided, quick; and in particular the little drops with which her laugh ended – three diminishing ahs . . . 'Ah-all-all . . .' I sometimes end a laugh that way myself . . .

VIRGINIA WOOLF (1882–1941)

Song for a Young Mother

There, there, you fit my lap
Like an acorn to its cup,
Your weight upon my arm
Is like a golden plum,
Like an apple in the hand
Or a stone on the ground.

As a bird in the fallow
scoops a shallow hollow
Where the earth's upward pressing
Answers egg and nestling
   Earth's mass and beginning
Of all their learning –

So you learn from my arm
You have substance and a house
So I learn from your birth
that I am not vague and wild
But as solid as my child
And as constant as the earth.

E. J. SCOVELL (1907–99)

Generations

What the daughter does, the mother did

JEWISH PROVERB

Comforted

As one whom his mother comforted, so will I comfort you . . .

SONG OF SOLOMON, 66: 13

To My Daughter Cathy

. . . You can go
Without regret
Away from this
Familiar land,
Leaving your kiss
Upon my hair
And all the future
In your hands

MARGARET MEAD (1901–78)

from Village Voice

What was locked in that extremity of expression that I so loved as a child? When the grown-ups became annoyed with our childish fights and shrieks and sent us out of the house yelling, 'Go play in the traffic!' Why did I feel deeply secure, certain of their undying love? Was it that by their yelling, their faces puffing red, their fingers pointing dramatically toward the door, their hateful words screaming out at the tops of their lungs, that I knew how much they loved us? Yes, it was that. But it was more. I sensed, I know, that they, by their own expression, acknowledged the devil in us all, established their toleration for the reality of our humanness. 'You are my hell on earth, my endless burden!' the mother shrieks at the child she patently adores. And the child, if not the neighbours, hears the silent addition: 'my reason for staying alive.'

JANE LAZARRE

from Revelations

No matter how old a mother is she watches her middle-aged children for signs of improvement.

FLORIDA SCOTT-MAXWELL (1883–1979)

from Of Woman Born

All human life on the planet is born of woman. The one unifying, incontrovertible experience shared by all women and men is that months-long period we spent unfolding inside a woman's body . . . Most of us first know both love and disappointment, power and tenderness, in the person of a woman. We carry the imprint of this experience for life, even into our dying.

ADRIENNE RICH (1929–)

Outside Your Body

Making the decision to have a child – it's momentous. It is to decide forever to have your heart go walking around outside your body.

ELIZABETH STONE

Loving Gaze

In the eyes of its mother every beetle is a gazelle.

MEXICAN PROVERB

FATHER LOVE

from Two Women

MY GIRL

As she grew and changed, I was increasingly wondering what this new girl could be, with her ecstatic adorations and rages. The beaming knife-keen awakening, cracking the dawn like an egg, her furies at the small frets of living, the long fat slumbers, almost continental in their reaches, the bedtimes of chuckles, private jokes and languors.

And who was I to her? The rough dark shadow of pummelling games and shouts, the cosy frightener, the tossing and swinging arms, lifting the body to the highest point of hysteria before lowering it back again to the safe male smell.

But she was my girl now, the second force in my life, and with her puffed, knowing eyes, forever moving with colour and light, she was well aware of it.

LAURIE LEE (1914–97)

from Dombey and Son

Dombey sat in the corner of the darkened room in the great armchair by the bedside, and Son lay tucked up warm in a little basket bedstead, carefully disposed on a low settee immediately in front of the fire and close to it, as if his constitution were analogous to that of a muffin, and it was essential to toast him brown while he was very new.

Dombey was about eight-and-forty years of age. Son about eight-and-forty minutes. Dombey was rather bald, rather red, and though a handsome well-made man, too stern and pompous in appearance to be prepossessing. Son was very bald, and very red, and though (of course) an undeniably fine infant, somewhat crushed and spotty in his general effect, as yet. On the brow of Dombey, Time and his brother Care had set some marks, as on a tree that was to come down in good time – remorseless twins they are for striding through their human forests, notching as they go – while the countenance of Son was crossed with a thousand little creases, which the same deceitful Time would take delight in smoothing out and wearing away with the flat part of his scythe, as a preparation of the surface for his deeper operations.

Dombey, exulting in the long-looked-for event, jingled and jingled the heavy gold watch-chain that depended from below his trim blue coat, whereof the buttons sparkled phosphorescently in the feeble rays of the distant fire. Son, with his little fists curled up and clenched, seemed, in his feeble way, to be squaring at existence for having come upon him so unexpectedly.

CHARLES DICKENS (1812–70)

from Wishes to My Son, John

For this new, and all succeeding years:
January 1, 1630

If wishes may enrich my boy,
My Jack, that art thy father's joy,
They shall be showered upon thy head
As thick as manna, angels' bread:
And bread I wish thee – this short word
Will furnish both thy back and board.

May a pure soul inhabit still
This well mixed clay, and a straight will
Biased by reason, that by grace.
May gems of price maintain their place
In such a casket: in that list
Chaste turquoise, sober amethyst.

Peace I do wish thee from those wars
Which gownmen talk out at the bars
Four times a year: I wish thee peace
Of conscience, country, and increase
In all that best of men commends,
Favour with God, good men thy friends.
Last, for lasting legacy
I this bequeath, when thou shalt die,
Heaven's monarch bless mine eyes, to see
My wishes crowned, in crowning thee.

HENRY KING (1592–1669)

Early Morning Feed

The father darts out on the stairs
To listen to that keening
In the upper room, for a change of note
That signifies distress, to scotch disaster,
The kettle humming in the room behind.

He thinks, on tiptoe, ears-a-strain,
The cool dawn rising like the moon:
'Must not appear and pick him up;
He mustn't think he has me springing
To his beck and call,'
The kettle rattling behind the kitchen door.

He has him springing
A-quiver on the landing –
For a distress-note, a change of key,
To gallop up the stairs to him
To take him up, light as a violin,
And stroke his back until he smiles.
He sidles in the kitchen
And pours his tea . . .

And again stands hearkening
For milk cracking the lungs.
There's a little panting,
A cough: the thumb's in: he'll sleep,
The cup of tea cooling on the kitchen table.

Can he go in now to his chair and think
Of the miracle of breath, pick up a book,
Ready at all times to take it at a run
And intervene between him and disaster,
Sipping his cold tea as the sun comes up?

He returns to bed
And feels like something, with the door ajar,
Crouched in the bracken, alert, with big eyes
For the hunter, death, disaster.

PETER REDGROVE (1932–2003)

The Toys

My little Son, who looked from thoughtful eyes,
And moved and spoke in quiet grown-up wise,
Having my law the seventh time disobeyed,
I struck him, and dismissed
With hard words and unkissed,
– His Mother, who was patient, being dead.
Then, fearing lest his grief should hinder sleep,
I visited his bed,
But found him slumbering deep,
With darkened eyelids, and their lashes yet
From his late sobbing wet.
And I, with moan,
Kissing away his tears, left others of my own;
For on a table drawn beside his head,
He had put, within his reach,
A box of counters and a red-veined stone,
A piece of glass abraded by the beach,
And six or seven shells,
A bottle with bluebells,
And two French copper coins, ranged there with careful art,
To comfort his sad heart.
So when that night I prayed
To God, I wept, and said:
Ah, when at last we lie with tranced breath,
Not vexing Thee in death,
And Thou rememberest of what toys
We made our joys,
How weakly understood
Thy great commanded good,
Then fatherly not less
Than I whom Thou has moulded from the clay,
Thou'lt leave Thy wrath, and say,
'I will be sorry for their childishness.'

COVENTRY PATMORE (1823–96)

Sonnet: To a Friend Who Asked, How I Felt When the Nurse First Presented My Infant to Me

Charles! my slow heart was only sad, when first
    I scanned that face of feeble infancy:
For dimly on my thoughtful spirit burst
    All I had been, and all my child might be!
But when I saw it on its mother's arm,
    And hanging at her bosom (she the while
    Bent o'er its features with a tearful smile)
Then I was thrilled and melted, and most warm
Impressed a father's kiss: and all beguiled
    Of dark remembrance and presageful fear,
    I seemed to see an angel-form appear –
'Twas even thine, beloved woman mild!
    So for the mother's sake the child was dear,
And dearer was the mother for the child.

SAMUEL TAYLOR COLERIDGE (1772–1834)

A Poet's Welcome to His Love-begotten Daughter; the First Instance That Entitled Him to the Venerable Appelation of Father

Thou's welcome, wean! Mischanter fa' me,
If thoughts o' thee, or yet thy Mamie,
Shall ever daunton me or awe me,
My bonie lady;
Or if I blush when thou shalt ca' me
Tyta, or Daddie.

Though now they ca' me fornicator,
And tease my name in kintra clatter,
The mair they talk, I'm kend the better;
E'en let them clash!
An auld wife's tongue's a feckless matter
To gie ane fash.

Welcome! My bonie, sweet wee dochter!
Though ye come here a wee unsought for;
And though your comin I hae fought for,
Baith Kirk and Queir;
Yet by my faith, ye're no unwrought for,
That I shall swear!

Wee image o' my bonie Betty,
As fatherly I kiss and daut thee,
As dear and near my heart I set thee,
Wi' as gude will,
As a' the Priests had seen me get thee
That's out o' h—.

Sweet fruit o' monie a merry dint,
My funny toil is no a' tint;
Though ye come to the warld asklent,

Which fools may scoff at,
In my last plack your part's be in't,
        The better half o't.

Though I should be the waur bestead,
Thou's be as braw and bienly clad,
And thy young years as nicely bred
        Wi' education,
As any brat o' Wedlock's bed,
        In a' thy station.

Lord grant that thou may ay inherit
Thy Mither's looks an' gracefu' merit;
An' thy poor, worthless Daddie's spirit,
        Without his failins!
'Twad please me mair to see thee heir it
        Than stocked mailins!

For if thou be, what I wad hae thee,
And tak the counsel I shall gie thee,
I'll never rue my trouble wi' thee,
        The cost nor shame o't,
But be a loving Father to thee,
        And brag the name o't.

ROBERT BURNS (1759–96)

from Frost at Midnight

Dear Babe, that sleepest cradled by my side,
Whose gentle breathings, heard in this deep calm,
Fill up the intersperséd vacancies
And momentary pauses of the thought!
My babe so beautiful! it thrills my heart
With tender gladness, thus to look at thee,
And think that thou shalt learn far other lore,
And in far other scenes! For I was reared
In the great city, pent 'mid cloisters dim,
And saw nought lovely but the sky and stars.
But *thou*, my babe! shalt wander like a breeze
By lakes and sandy shores, beneath the crags
Of ancient mountain, and beneath the clouds,
Which image in their bulk both lakes and shores
And mountain crags: so shalt thou see and hear
The lovely shapes and sounds intelligible
Of that eternal language, which they God
Utters, who from eternity doth teach
Himself in all, and all things in himself.
Great universal Teacher! he shall mold
Thy spirit, and by giving make it ask.

Therefore all seasons shall be sweet to thee,
Whether the summer clothe the general earth
With greenness, or the redbreast sit and sing
Betwixt the tufts of snow on the bare branch
Of mossy apple tree, while the nigh thatch
Smokes in the sun-thaw; whether the eave-drops fall
Heard only in the trances of the blast,
Or if the secret ministry of frost
Shall hang them up in silent icicles,
Quietly shining to the quiet Moon.

SAMUEL TAYLOR COLERIDGE (1772–1834)

On My First Son

Farewell, thou child of my right hand, and joy;
   My sin was too much hope of thee, lov'd boy.
Seven years thou wert lent to me, and I thee pay,
   Exacted by thy fate, on the just day.
Oh, could I lose all father now! For why
   Will man lament the state he should envy?
To have so soon 'scaped world's and flesh's rage,
   And if no other misery, yet age!
Rest in soft peace, and, asked, say, Here doth lie
   Ben Jonson his best piece of poetry.
For whose sake henceforth all his vows be such
   As what he loves may never like too much.

BEN JONSON (1572–1637)

A Father's Lullaby

Lullaby, oh, lullaby!
Thus I heard a father cry,
Lullaby, oh, lullaby!
That brat will never shut an eye;
Hither come, some power divine!
Close his lids or open mine!

Lullaby, oh, lullaby!
What the devil makes him cry?
Lullaby, oh, lullaby!
Still he stares – I wonder why?
Why are not the sons of earth
Blind, like puppies, from the birth?

Lullaby, oh, lullaby!
Thus I heard the father cry;
Lullaby, oh, Lullaby!
Mary, you must come and try! –
Hush, oh, hush, for mercy's sake –
The more I sing, the more you wake!

Lullaby, oh, lullaby!
Two such nights, and I shall die!
Lullaby, oh, lullaby!
He'll be bruised, and so shall I, –
How can I from bedposts keep,
When I'm walking in my sleep?

THOMAS HOOD (1779–1845)

Those Winter Sundays

Sundays too my father got up early
and put his clothes on in the blueblack cold,
then with cracked hands that ached
from labor in the weekday weather made
banked fires blaze. No one ever thanked him.

I'd wake and hear the cold splintering, breaking.
When the rooms were warm, he'd call,
and slowly I would rise and dress,
fearing the chronic angers of that house,

Speaking indifferently to him,
who had driven out the cold
and polished my good shoes as well.
What did I know, what did I know
of love's austere and lonely offices?

ROBERT HAYDEN (1913–80)

Mater Triumphans

Son of my woman's body, you go, to the drum and fife,
To taste the colour of love and the other side of life –
From out of the dainty the rude, the strong from out of
the frail,
Eternally through the ages from the female comes the
male.

The ten fingers and toes, and the shell-like nail on
each,
The eyes blind as gems and the tongue attempting
speech;
Impotent hands in my bosom, and yet they shall
wield the sword!
Drugged with slumber and milk, you wait the day of the
Lord.

Infant bridegroom, uncrowned King, unanointed
priest,
Soldier, lover, explorer, I see you nuzzle the breast.
You that grope in my bosom shall load the ladies with
rings,
You, that came forth through the doors, shall burst the
doors of kings.

ROBERT LOUIS STEVENSON (1850–94)

from How a Real Man Became a Real Dad

You can go to movies, and the park, and the ball game, and Disneyland, and the moon for all it matters, but if you really want to spend the day with your child, just . . .

. . . be there.

Look around, and if you can find a spot on the floor that is not covered with toys, sit on it. Pick up the nearest doll, and say, in your most robotic voice, 'I am the doll from the planet Blobby. I have just come to this planet. Can you please tell me what dolls do on your planet?'

Your child will take it from there. All the other dolls, and cars, and balls, and blocks, will be invited to meet and instruct the doll from the planet Blobby.

You should listen. You will learn a few things.

This game may start to pale, for you, in a few minutes. It will not, for your child.

Hang in there.

Dads are used to looking forward, five minutes. We will be happy when the groceries are put away, when this report is filed, when this mess is cleaned up. Your child is trying to teach you what Baba Ram Dass could not. Ram Dass was Richard Alpert, the Harvard professor who got kicked out for experimenting with LSD with Timothy Leary and writing about it. His seminal work, *Be Here Now*, tried to teach a generation about a more simple, spiritual way of life, a way of being in the moment.

Which is exactly what your kid is trying to teach you when he refuses to get out of the bathtub, or get in the car, or end an endless game of Doll from Planet Blobby. Your child is in the moment and of the moment. This is why kids both refuse to get into the bathtub, and to get out of it. Why would a dry person want to be wet? Dry is the perfect state. And, later: Why would a wet person want to be dry? Wet is the perfect state.

And, of course, why would I want to stop playing Doll from Planet Blobby? There is no other game. This is the game.

PHILIP LERMAN

My Baby

Loveliness beyond completeness,
Sweetness distancing all sweetness,
Beauty all that beauty may be –
That's May Bennett, that's my baby.

WILLIAM COX BENNETT (1820–95)

On the Birth of His Daughter Valentine

It's a girl . . . a little beauty, an angel, and I'm madly in love
with her.

HENRY MILLER (1891–1980)

Parting

Then farewell, my dear; my loved daughter, adieu;
The last pang of life is in parting from you.

THOMAS JEFFERSON (1743–1826)

GAMES TO PLAY
WITH BABIES

How Many Days Has My Baby to Play?

How many days has my baby to play?
Saturday, Sunday, Monday
Tuesday, Wednesday, Thursday, Friday
Saturday, Sunday, Monday.

Hop away, skip away,
My baby wants to play,
My baby wants to play every day.

TRADITIONAL

137

Round and Round the Garden

Round and round the garden
Like a teddy bear.
One step, two step,
Tickle you under there!

TRADITIONAL

Gently trace around the palm of the baby's hand, travel up the arm in two movements then tickle under the arm.

Little Pigs

This little piggy went to market,
This little piggy stayed at home,
This little pig had roast beef,
This little pig had none,
And this little pig cried:
Wee-wee-wee- wee- wee-wee,
All the way home!

TRADITIONAL

Count from big toe to little toe then end with a tickle to the feet or tummy.

Dance, Thumbkin, Dance

Dance, Thumbkin, dance,
Dance, you merry men, every one:
But Thumbkin, he can dance alone,
Thumbkin, he can dance. Dance, Pointer, dance . . .
Dance, Longman, dance . . .
Dance, Ringman, dance . . .
Dance, Baby, dance . . .

TRADITIONAL

Waggle the baby's thumb, tucking four fingers into palm, then let all the fingers move. Do this with each finger in turn.

Handy Pandy

Handy Pandy,
Sugar Candy,
Which one will you choose,
Top or bottom?

TRADITIONAL

Hide something in a closed fist; put the other fist above or below. The child chooses which hand.

Pat-a-Cake

Pat-a-Cake, pat-a-cake, baker's man,
Bake me a cake as fast as you can;
Pat it and prick it and mark it with B.
Put it in the oven for baby and me.

TRADITIONAL

Act out pricking the baby's palm and tracing a B. Can also be a clapping song.

Two Little Dicky Birds

Two little dicky birds,
Sitting on a wall,
One named Peter,
One named Paul.
Fly away, Peter!
Fly away, Paul!
Come back, Peter!
Come back, Paul!

TRADITIONAL

Show a finger from each hand to represent the birds, then one disappears behind the back, then the other; then one returns, then the other.

This Is the Way the Ladies Ride

This is the way the ladies ride,
Nimble-nim, nimble-nim;

This is the way the gentlemen ride,
Gallop-a-trot! Gallop-a-trot!

This is the way the farmers ride,
Jiggety-jog, jiggery-jog;

This is the way the butcher boy rides,
Tripperty-trot, tripperty trot,

Till he falls in a ditch with a flipperty,
Flipperty, flop, flop, FLOP!

TRADITIONAL

The baby rides on the knee, the movement imitating the different ways of riding, until at the end there is a sudden, delightful, drop between your knees.

FOOT RIDE

Rigadoon

Rigadoon, rigadoon,
Now let him fly,
Sit him on father's foot,
Jump him up high.

Cross your ankles, and sit the baby astride them. Swing gently up and down.

Ride a Cock-Horse to Banbury Cross

Ride a cock-horse to Banbury Cross,
To see a fine lady upon a white horse;
Rings on her fingers.
And bells on her toes,
She shall have music
    wherever she goes.

A Trot, a Canter

A trot, a canter,
A gallop and over,
Out of the saddle
And roll in the clover.

Happy

If you're happy and you know it, clap your hands,
If you're happy and you know it, clap your hands,
If you're happy and you know it and you really want to
     show it,
If you're happy and you know it, clap your hands.

If you're happy and you know it, stamp your feet,
If you're happy and you know it, nod your head,
If you're happy and you know it, shout 'Hooray' . . .

TRADITIONAL

Miss Polly

Miss Polly had a dolly who was sick, sick, sick,
So she phoned for the doctor to be quick, quick, quick.
The doctor came with her bag and her hat,
And she knocked on the door with a rat-a-tat-tat.

She looked at the dolly and she shook her head,
And she said, 'Miss Polly, put her straight to bed.'
She wrote on a paper for a pill, pill, pill,
'I'll be back in the morning with my bill, bill, bill.'

TRADITIONAL

Jelly on the Plate

Jelly on the plate,
Jelly on the plate,
Wibble wobble,
Wibble wobble,
Jelly on the plate.
(*Wobble the baby from side to side.*)

Sweeties in the jar.
Sweeties in the jar.
Shake them up,
Shake them up,
Sweeties in the jar.
(*Shake up and down gently*)

Fire on the floor,
Stamp it out,
Stamp it out,
Fire on the floor.
(*Bounce the baby to the ground and up again.*)

Candles on the cake,
Candles on the cake,
Blow them out,
Blow them out,
Puff puff puff.
(*Blow at each other*)

TRADITIONAL

What Shall We Do With a Lazy Katie?

What shall we do with a lazy Katie? (*or whatever the name of the*
  child is)
What shall we do with a lazy Katie?
What shall we do with a lazy Katie,
Early in the morning?

Roll her on the bed and tickle her all over,
Roll her on the bed and tickle her all over,
Roll her on the bed and tickle her all over,
Early in the morning.

Heave ho and UP she rises,
Heave ho and UP she rises,
Heave ho and UP she rises,
Early in the morning

TRADITIONAL

Sing to the tune of 'What shall we do with the drunken sailor?' Follow the
words of the song: roll her or him on the bed, tickle and lift up.

The Baby's Dance

Dance, little baby, dance up high:
Never mind, baby, mother is by;
Crow and caper, caper and crow,
There, little baby, there you go;
Up to the ceiling, down to the ground,
Backwards and forwards, round and round:
Dance, little baby, and mother shall sing,
With the merry gay coral, ding,
ding-a-ding, ding.

ANN TAYLOR (1782–1866)

Jack-in-the-Box Jumps UP Like This

Jack-in-the-box jumps UP like this,
He makes me laugh when he waggles his head,
I gently press him down again,
But Jack-in-the-box jumps UP instead.

TRADITIONAL

Raise the baby up, gently shake, lower down, then lift up quickly again.

Row On

Row, row, row your boat,
Gently down the stream,
Merrily, merrily, merrily,
Life is but a dream.

TRADITIONAL

*Rock babies from side to side. Older ones can be lifted up to sitting position
then back again, rocking back and forth.*

Can You?

Can you walk on tiptoe
As softly as a cat?

Can you stamp along the road
STAMP, STAMP, just like that?

Can you take some great big strides,
Just like a giant can?

Can you walk along so slowly,
Like a bent old man?

TRADITIONAL

Teddy Bear

Teddybear, teddybear,
dance on your toes.

Teddybear, teddybear,
touch your nose.

Teddybear, teddybear
stand on your head

Teddybear, teddybear
go to bed.

Teddybear, teddybear,
wake up now.

Teddybear, teddybear,
make your bow.

Teddybear, teddybear,
touch the ground.

Teddybear, teddybear,
turn right around.

Teddybear, teddybear,
run upstairs.

Teddybear, teddybear,
say your prayers.

Teddybear, teddybear,
turn off the light.

Teddybear, teddybear
say goodnight.

TRADITIONAL

Humpty Dumpty Sat on a Wall

Humpty Dumpty sat on a wall
Humpty Dumpty had a great fall;
All the King's horses,
And all the King's men,
Couldn't put Humpty together again.

TRADITIONAL

Ring-a-Ring o'Roses

Ring-a-ring o'Roses,
A pocket full of posies,
A-tishoo! A-tishoo!
We all fall down

The cows are in the meadow
Eating buttercups,
A-tishoo! A-Tishoo!
We all get up.

TRADITIONAL

Five Brown Teddies Sitting on a Wall

Five brown teddies sitting on a wall,
Five brown teddies sitting on a wall,
And if one brown teddy should accidentally fall,
There'd be four brown teddies sitting on a wall.

Four brown teddies sitting on a wall . . .
Three brown teddies sitting on a wall . . .
Two brown teddies sitting on a wall . . .
One brown teddy sitting on a wall,
One brown teddy sitting on a wall,
And if one brown teddy should accidentally fall,
There'd be no brown teddies sitting there at all!

TRADITIONAL

Sing to the tune of 'Ten Green Bottles'.

SONG GAMES

Rub-a-Dub-Dub, Three Men in a Tub

Rub-a-dub-dub, three men in a tub
And who do you think they be?
The butcher, the baker, the candlestick maker,
And my little (*fill in name of child, especially good if ends with e sound.*)

TRADITIONAL

There Were Five in the Bed

There were five in the bed and
the little one said: Roll over! Roll over!
So they all rolled over and one fell out.
There were four in the bed . . .
There were three in the bed . . .
There were two in the bed . . .

There was one in the bed,
And that little one said:
Good, now I've got the bed to myself, I'm going to
    stretch and stretch and stretch!

TRADITIONAL

Here We Go Round the Mulberry Bush

Here we go round the mulberry bush
the mulberry bush, the mulberry bush.
Here we go round the mulberry bush.
On a cold and frosty morning.

Join hands and dance in a circle. Stop to do the actions of the next verses,
repeating the first verse and its dance after each one.

This is the way we wash our hands,
Wash our hands, wash our hands,
This is the way we wash our hands,
On a cold and frosty morning.

This is the way we wash our face . . .
This is the way we brush our hair . . .
This is the way we clean our teeth . . .
This is the way we put on our clothes . . .

TRADITIONAL

A NEW VOICE

from The First Year

The baby in her blue nightjacket, propped on hands
With head raised, coming out to day, has half-way
   sloughed
The bed-clothes, as a sea-lion, as a mermaid
Half sloughs the sea, rooted in sea, basking on strands

Like a gentle coastal creature she looks round
At one who comes and goes the far side of her bars;
Firm in her place and lapped by blankets; here like tides
Familiar rise and care for her, our sounds.

E. J. SCOVELL (1907–99)

A Baby's Hands

A baby's hands, like rosebuds furled
Whence yet no leaf expands,
Ope if you touch, though close upcurled,
A baby's hands.

Then, fast as warriors grip their brands
When battle's bolt is hurled,
They close, clenched hard like tightening bands.

No rosebuds yet by dawn impearled
Match, even in loveliest lands,
The sweetest flowers in all the world –
A baby's hands.

ALGERNON CHARLES SWINBURNE (1837–1909)

She Is Learning Her Hands

She is learning her hands
like a flute player
with the little finger perched
on an inch of thin air
above the last stop.

She is playing arpeggios slowly,
each finger depressing
a hammer of air
onto silence.
She has perfect pitch.

She is examining the find
of her hand's back,
levelled for the light's fall,
her rosetta stone
with the clue to creation.

She is closing her hands
on the feel of her fingers,
discovering cushions of palm,
seeing how far you can come
without skin touching.

She is tucking her thumb
between index and middle finger,
cat's tongue
left out when she curls into sleep.

She is learning the space
between what the eyes see
and the hands grasp,
assured of an arm's length
five fingers' dimensions.

She is timeing the gaps
within touch,
testing one hand with another,
finding what touches is touched,
like a lover.

DESMOND GRAHAM (1940–)

Seated

At seven months you sit on cold tiles
and don't keel over. You've found
the ground like a sail-boat at low tide,
dragged to mudflats. You're puzzled;

a sailor stepping onto a dock, dizzy
but met by land's intransigence. Your arms
and smile wave to me, the room's tipped
the right way up, and nothing gives.

Your bones know shunting now,
the finite pile-up of sensation on
sensation. You chuck your rattle down,
sombrely note that staccato *clack*.

You begin to know the lust for water,
how it fractures objects, warps, but holds.
Your arms implore me, *Mama!* and I sweep
you onto the ballast of my shoulder.

SALLY READ (1971–)

Dimples

I know a baby, such a baby, –
Round blue eyes and cheeks of pink,
Such an elbow furrowed with dimples,
Such a wrist where creases sink.

'Cuddle and love me, cuddle and love me,'
Crows the mouth of coral pink:
Oh the bald head, and oh the sweet lips,
And oh the sleepy eyes that wink!

The Very Thing for Kisses

My baby has a mottled fist,
My baby has a neck in creases;
My baby kisses and is kissed,
For he's the very thing for kisses.

CHRISTINA ROSSETTI (1830–94)

from Aurora Leigh

There he lay upon his back,
The yearling creature, warm and moist with life
To the bottom of his dimples – and to the ends
Of the lovely tumbled curls about his face;
For since he had been covered over-much
To keep him from the light-glare, both his cheeks
Were hot and scarlet as the first live rose
The shepherd's heart-blood ebbed away into
The faster for his love. And love was here
As instant; in the pretty baby-mouth,
Shut close as if for dreaming that it sucked,
The little naked feet, drawn up the way
Of nestled birdlings; everything so soft
And tender – to the tiny holdfast hands
Which, closing on a finger into sleep,
Had kept a mould of't.

Elizabeth Barrett Browning (1806–61)

from Still Life

William grew, stretched, changed shape. This seemed to happen in the twinkling of an eye and with the luxurious slowness with which he himself would examine the progress of a caterpillar. The feeble hands that clutched became square, gluey exploring fingers that could pick up the smallest crumb. The jerking bowed legs became massively creased and then, used, grew to muscle. Stephanie watched his vertebrae expand. He sat on the ground and beat it with a skittle, a blue beaker. He lay grounded for weeks on his Buddha-belly and then one day was up, swaying precariously like Blake's Nebuchadnezzar on purposeful hands and untouched, soft-skinned knees. He went rapidly backwards, focusing on a coalscuttle, butting against a bookcase on the other side of the room. He stood, with wavering hands and jack-knifing knees. He walked, from skirt to chair, moving slowly round the room, clutching and puffing, raising his plump foot high and planting it. She thought she would never forget any of these moments, these points of development, these markers in time, and forgot all of them as the next stage seemed to be William and eternal . . .

He would sit on her knee and look at her face, testing her contours with fingers that in the early days, judging distances, jabbed at a bright eye or clawed at a lip-corner, and grew rapidly skilled at caressing, patting her cheek, tangling her hair. She saw herself in him: the learning face was her face. They looked into each other's eyes and she saw herself reflected, a looming light, a loving moon, part of himself? His flesh was her flesh, but his look was not her look . . .

She would hold him up, when he cried, to window or lamp, saying, 'There, Will, look at the light, look at the light.'

And very early in his life he would repeat ''igh, 'igh.' She taught him also early book, cat, flower and he applied these names extensively, using 'boo' of pictures and newspapers, 'cat' of all animals, and 'fowa' of vegetables, trees, feathers and once of his grandmother's modesty-front, poking out of the neck of her dress. He sat regally on Stephanie's knee and named farmyards and jungles of pictured beasts, cow, hoss, gog, 'en, zeb-a, effunt, 'nake, 'raffe, whale. These things are banal enough and it is hard to write the wonder with which, in a mood of distance from the everyday and the solid, a woman can hear a voice speak where there has only been a wail, a snuffle, a cry, a mutter of syllables. Will's voice was a *new* voice, speaking words that had been spoken generation after generation. Look at the light. I love you.

A. S. BYATT (1936–)

from Love Forty

It was an extraordinary moment: something electric.
It was as if somebody had just come into the room.
Up till now, we'd admired her quiet alertness
and her wakeful curiosity, but had received from her
nothing but a rather stern stare. It was as if, all at once,
she was a person at last: had joined us.
This smile wreathed itself about my heart.
It was the moment of a lifetime, never to be forgotten.

SUE LIMB (1946–)

from My Diary

Unexpected pleasure has occasionally made her cry: seeing her Papa after an absence of a few days; and I thought tears were not a common manifestation of joy in children so young, not thirteen months old yet . . . She is very *feminine* I think, in her quietness, which is as far removed from inactivity of mind as possible. She sits on the ground much more than she did, amusing herself pretty well (this amusing *herself*, has been, I fear, more my theory than my practice). I do not think she shows much perseverance, otherwise she would try longer to reach her playthings herself, etc, but this *may be* bodily inability . . .

She dislikes *finishing* her food and, by a curious sort of fancy, often refuses the last two or three spoonfuls through dread of coming to the bottom . . .

We have been puzzled for a punishment. The usual one, putting the little offender into a corner, had no effect with her, as she made it into a game to 'I *do* into a corner and be naughty little girl . . .'

She is very touching in her sweet little marks of affection. Once or twice, when I have seemed unhappy about little things, she has come and held up her sweet mouth to be kissed. Last night I was in pain, and made a sort of moan. She was lying by me, apparently asleep; but as if her gentle instinct of love prompted her even then, she pressed to me, saying, 'Kiss, Mama.' These are trifles, but how very precious may the remembrance of them become . . .

ELIZABETH GASKELL (1810–65)

from The Haunted Man

It was a peculiarity of this baby to be always cutting teeth. Whether they never came, or whether they came and went away again, is not in evidence; but it had certainly cut enough, on the showing of Mrs Tetterby, to make a handsome dental provision for the sign of the Bull and Mouth . . . Mrs Tetterby always said, 'it was coming through, and then the child would be herself'; and still it never did come through, and the child continued to be somebody else.

CHARLES DICKENS (1812–70)

It Must Be the Milk

There is a thought that I have tried not to but cannot help but
  think,
Which is, My goodness how much infants resemble people who
  have had too much to drink.
Tots and sots, so different and yet so identical!
What a humiliating coincidence for pride parentical!
Yet when you see your little dumpling set sail across the nursery
  floor,
Can you conscientiously deny the resemblance to somebody who is
  leaving a tavern after having tried to leave it a dozen times and
  each time turned back for just one more?
Each step achieved
Is simply too good to be believed;
Foot somehow follows foot
And somehow manages to stay put;
Arms wildly semaphore,
Wild eyes seem to ask, Whatever did we get in such a dilemma for?
And their gait is more that of a duckling than a Greek goddessling or
  godling,
And in inebriates it's called staggering but in infants it's called
  toddling.
Another kinship with topers is also by infants exhibited,
Which is that they are completely uninhibited,
And they can't talk straight
Any more than they can walk straight;
Their pronunciation is awful
And their grammar is flawful,
And in adults it's drunken and maudlin and deplorable,
But in infants it's tunnin' and adorable.
So I hope you will agree that it is very hard to tell an infant from
  somebody who has gazed too long into the cup,
And really the only way you can tell them apart is to wait till next
  day, and the infant is the one that feels all right when it wakes up.

Ogden Nash (1902–71)

Frog-like

An ugly baby is a very nasty object – and the prettiest is frightful when undressed – till about four months; in short as long as they have their big body and little limbs and that terrible frog-like action.

QUEEN VICTORIA TO THE PRINCESS ROYAL,
2 May 1859 (1819–1901)

SLEEPY LOVE SONGS

Beautiful Boy

Close your eyes,
Have no fear,
The monsters gone,
He's on the run and your daddy's here,

Beautiful,
Beautiful, beautiful,
Beautiful Boy,

Before you go to sleep,
Say a little prayer,
Every day in every way,
It's getting better and better,

Beautiful,
Beautiful, beautiful,
Beautiful Boy,

Out on the ocean sailing away,
I can hardly wait,
To see you come of age,
But I guess we'll both,
Just have to be patient,
'Cause it's a long way to go,
A hard row to hoe,
Yes, it's a long way to go,
But in the meantime,

Before you cross the street,
Take my hand,
Life is just what happens to you,
While you're busy making other plans,

Beautiful,
Beautiful, beautiful,
Beautiful Boy,
Darling,
Darling,
Darling Sean.

JOHN LENNON (1940–80)

Hush-a-Bye Baby

Hush-a-bye baby
On the tree top.
When the wind blows,
The cradle will rock;
When the bough breaks,
The cradle will fall;
Down will come baby,
Cradle and all.

TRADITIONAL

Bye Low, Bye Low

Bye low, bye low,
Baby's in the cradle sleeping;
Tip toe, tip toe.
Still as pussy slyly creeping;
Bye low, bye low,
Rock the cradle, baby's waking;
Hush, my baby, oh!

TRADITIONAL

Brahms' Lullaby

Lullaby and goodnight.
With lilies of white
And roses of red
To pillow your head:
May you wake when the day
Chases darkness away,
May you wake when the day
Chases darkness away.

Lullaby and goodnight,
Let angels of light
Spread wings round your bed
And guard you from dread.
Slumber gently and deep
In the dreamland of sleep,
Slumber gently and deep
In the dreamland of sleep.

JOHANNES BRAHMS (1833–97)

The Dreamland Tree

Sleep, baby, sleep,
Thy father guards the sheep;
Thy mother shakes the dreamland tree
And from it fall sweet dreams for thee,
Sleep, baby, sleep.

HAITI, TRADITIONAL

I Pray to Allah

Oooo . . .
I pray to Allah, I pray to Allah
I shall capture for you a pair of pigeons
Don't fear little pigeons. I've said this only
To urge my little one to sleep
I pray to Allah, I pray to Allah
I shall capture for you, two chickens
Don't fear dear chickens. I've said this only
To urge my little one to sleep
I pray to Allah, I pray to Allah
I shall capture for you, two little chicks
Don't fear little chicks. I've said this only
So that my little one will now sleep
Oooo . . .

EGYPT, TRADITIONAL

Seal Lullaby

Oh! hush thee, my baby, the night is behind us,
  And black are the waters that sparkled so green.
The moon, o'er the combers, looks downward to find us
  At rest in the hollows that rustle between.
Where billow meets billow, there soft by the pillow;
  Ah, weary wee flipperling, curl at thy ease!
The storm shall not wake thee, nor shark overtake thee,
  Asleep in the arms of the slow-swinging seas.

RUDYARD KIPLING (1865–1936)

Chinese Lullaby

Chinese Sandman
Wise and creepy,
Croon dream-songs
To make me sleepy.

A Chinese maid with slanting eyes
Is queen of all their lullabies.
On her ancient moon-guitar
She strums a sleep-song to a star;
And when big China-shadows fall
Snow-white lilies hear her call

Chinese Sandman
Wise and creepy,
Croon dream-songs
To make us sleepy.

ANONYMOUS

A Frog He Would A-Wooing Go

A frog he would a-wooing go, m–m, m–m,
A frog he would a-wooing go,
Whether his mother would let him or no, m–m, m–m.

He rode right to Miss Mousie's den, m–m, m–m,
He rode right to Miss Mousie's den,
Said he, 'Miss Mousie, are you within?' m–m, m–m.

'Yes, kind Sir Frog, I sit to spin,' m–m, m–m,
'Yes, kind Sir Frog, I sit to spin.
Pray, Mister Frog, won't you walk in?' m–m, m–m.

He said, 'My dear, I've come to see,' m–m, m–m,
He said, 'My dear, I've come to see,
If you, Miss Mousie, will marry me?' m–m, m–m.

'I don't know what to say to that,' m–m, m–m,
'I don't know what to sav to that,
Till I can see my Uncle Rat.' m–m, m–m.

When Uncle Rat came riding home, m–m, m–m,
When Uncle Rat came riding home,
Said he, 'Who's been here since I've been gone?' m–m, m–m.

'A fine young gentleman has been here,' m–m, m–m,
'A fine young gentleman has been here,
Who wants to marry me, it is clear.' m–m, m–m.

So Uncle Rat he rode to town, m–m, m–m,
So Uncle Rat he rode to town,
And bought his niece a wedding gown, m–m, m–m.

'Where shall our wedding supper be?' m–m, m–m,
'Where shall our wedding supper be?'
'Down in the trunk of some hollow tree.' m–m, m–m.

The first to come was a Bumblebee, m-m, m-m,
The first to come was a Bumblebee,
He strung his fiddle over his knee, m-m, m-m.

The next to come was the Captain Flea, m-m, m-m,
The next to come was the Captain Flea,
He danced a jig with the Bumblebee, m-m, m-m.

The next to come was the big Black Snake, m-m, m-m,
The next to come was the big Black Snake,
And on his head was the wedding cake, m-m. m-m.

The Frog and Mouse they went to France, m-m, m-m,
The Frog and Mouse they went to France,
And this is the story of their romance, m-m, m-m.

ANONYMOUS

Precious Roses

O Creator, O Creator,
Thou who puts children to sleep,
Make my little one sleep
Amid precious roses.
Make my little one sleep
Amid precious roses.

ANONYMOUS

The Lamb So Mild

Sleep, baby, sleep,
Our cottage vale is deep:
The little lamb is on the green,
With woolly fleece so soft and clean –
Sleep, baby, sleep.

Sleep, baby, sleep,
Down where the woodbines creep;
Be always like the lamb so mild,
A kind, and sweet, and gentle child.
Sleep, baby, sleep.

ANONYMOUS

A Baby's Boat

Baby's boat's a silver moon
Sailing in the sky.
Sailing o'er a sea of sleep
While the stars float by.

Sail, baby, sail
Out upon that sea;
Only don't forget to sail
Back again to me.

Baby's fishing for a dream,
Fishing far and near,
Her line a silver moonbeam is,
Her bait a silver star.

Sail, baby, sail
Out upon that sea;
Only don't forget to sail
Back again to me.

ANONYMOUS

A Blanket of Eye-Lashes

When my soul embraces you,
Its enchantment is increased,
Flower of thy mother's heart,
Sleep, my love, sleep.
O-O- my love sleep.

Don't cry my son,
I beseech thee,
Your weeping grieves
And torments me,
Sleep, O light of my eyes,
Don't trouble me,
A blanket are my eye-lashes
Woven for thee,
O-O- my love sleep.

Tonight your curls are luminous,
The star thus disappeared,
And your smiles shed light
Until daylight,
May God bless you.
Your home may He make lofty,
And may he increase its bounty,
With ostrich feather comfort.
O-O- my love sleep.

LEBANON, TRADITIONAL

Sweet and Low

Sweet and low, sweet and low.
    Wind of the western sea.
Low, low, breathe and blow,
    Wind of the western sea!
    Over the rolling waters go,
    Come from the dying moon, and blow,
    Blow him again to me;
While my little one, while my pretty one, sleeps.

Sleep and rest, sleep and rest,
    Father will come to thee soon;
Rest, rest, on mother's breast,
    Father will come to thee soon;
    Father will come to his babe in the nest,
    Silver sails all out of the west
    Under the silver moon;
Sleep, my little one, my pretty one, sleep.

ALFRED, LORD TENNYSON (1809–92)

Golden Slumbers Kiss Your Eyes

Golden slumbers kiss your eyes,
Smiles awake you when you rise.
Sleep, pretty wantons, do not cry,
And I will sing a lullaby:
Rock them, rock them, lullaby.

Care is heavy, therefore sleep you;
You are care, and care must keep you.
Sleep, pretty wantons, do not cry,
And I will sing a lullaby:
Rock them, rock them, lullaby.

THOMAS DEKKER (1572–1632)

ADVICE AND SAYINGS

from Baby and Child Care

Trust yourself. You know more than you think you do . . . It may surprise you to hear that the more people have studied different methods of bringing up children the more they have come to the conclusion that what good mothers and fathers instinctively feel like doing for their babies is usually best.

BENJAMIN SPOCK (1903–98)

Improvisation

There is no manual. Every day of being a parent is a constant improvisation.

JOSH BROLIN (1968–)

Disagreements

The problem is that the paediatrician disagrees with the health visitor who disagrees with the nurse who disagrees with your husband who disagrees with your mother-in-law who disagrees with your mother who disagrees with you. The answer is to agree with every one and do what agrees with the baby.

ANGELA LANSBURY (1925–)

from A Conversational Manual

LADY: Good morrow nurse.

NURSE: God give you good morrow, Madame.

LADY: How now, how doth the childe?

NURSE: He is fayre and plumpe, and doth very wel thanks be to God, saving that he hath been somewhat waiward the last night.

LADY: Hath he so? What shold ail him? It may be he hath some tooth a growing, is he in his cradle? See if he sleepeth.

NURSE: He is full awaken, Madame.

LADY: He is not yet made readie is he?

NURSE: No, Madame, I have let him sleepe all this morning.

LADY: Unswaddle him, undoe his swaddling bands, give him his brekefast while I am heere, make his pappe, take away that fier-brand that smoketh for it will taste of the smoke, where is his little spoone? Wash him before me, have you cleane water? O my little hart! God blesse thee. Rub the crowne of his head . . . 'What hath he upon his eyelid? Me thinks his eyes are somewhat watrish, make them cleane; how quick is his eyebal, hath he not a pimple upon his nose? His little cheeks are wet, I believe you did leave him alone to crye and weepe; picke his nostrils, wipe his mouth and his lips. How many teethe hath he? His gummes be sore. Showe me his tongue, let me see the pallet of his mouth, he hathe a prettie chin. What a fair necke he hath! Pull off his shirt, thou art prety and fat my little darling, wash his arme-pits; what ayleth his elboe? O what an arme he hath! His hand wrist is very small; open his right hand; the palme of his left hand is all on water, did he sweat? How he spreadeth his small fingers . . .

'You have not washed the insides nor the soles of his feete; forget not to make cleane his toes, the great toe and all, now swaddle him againe, but first put on his biggin, and his little band with an edge, where is his little petticoat? give him his coate of changeable taffeta, and his sattin sleeves; where is his bibbe? Let him have his gathered aprone with stringes, and hang a muckinder to it; you need not yet to give him his corall with the small golden chayne, for I beleeve it is better to let him sleepe till the afternoone. Give him some sucke . . .

'Set on the coverlet, now put him in his cradle and rocke him till he sleepe but bring him to me first that I may kisse him; God send thee good rest my little boykin. I pray you Nurse have a care of him.'

PETER ERONDELL (c.1550–1600)

from Alice in Wonderland

Speak roughly to your little boy
   And beat him when he sneezes:
He only does it to annoy
   Because he knows it teases

Chorus,
Wow! Wow! Wow!

I speak severely to my boy
   I beat him when he sneezes!
For he can thoroughly enjoy
   The pepper when he pleases!

Wow! Wow! Wow!

LEWIS CARROLL (1832–98)

Purpose

We think the purpose of a child is to grow up because it does grow up. But its purpose is to play, to enjoy itself, to be a child. If we merely look to the end of the process, the purpose of life is death.

ALEXANDER HERZEN (1812–70)

The Changeling

When larks gin sing
Away we fling,
And babes new-born steal as we go;
An elf instead
We leave in bed,
And wind out, laughing, Ho, Ho, Ho!

ANONYMOUS

To Her Eldest Daughter Vicki

TOO GREAT PASSION FOR VERY LITTLE BABIES

Stoneleigh Abbey, Kenilworth, June 15, 1858
. . . What you say of the pride of giving life to an immortal soul is
very fine, dear, but I own I cannot enter into that; I think much more
of our being like a cow or a dog at such moments; when our poor
nature becomes so very animal and unecstatic – but for you, dear, if
you are sensible and reasonable not in ecstasy nor spending your day
with nurses and wet nurses, which is the ruin of many a refined and
intellectual young lady, without adding to her real maternal duties, a
child will be a great resource . . . Think of me who at that first time,
very unreasonable, and perfectly furious as I was to be caught, having
to have drawing rooms and levees and made to sit down – and be
stared at and take every sort of precaution . . .

Buckingham Palace, June 22, 1858
You say I know you 'too well' to think you would spend your day in
a way unworthy of a lady and a princess – so I do, dear child, still I
know your rather too great passion for very little babies, and I wish
to guard you against overdoing the thing . . .

Balmoral Castle, October 1, 1858
Of all the wonderful German notions that one of a lady in your
condition being unable to stand godmother is the most extraordinary
I ever heard! . . . I have heard of so many christenings abroad where
people have been in that condition and stand as godmothers. I hope that
you will break through that; but above all promise me never to do so
improper and indecorous a thing as to be lying in a dressing gown on
a sofa at a christening! It would shock people here very much, and as
my daughter and an English Princess I expect you not do it . . .

Windsor Castle, November 17, 1858
I can not bear to think Bertie [Vicki's brother, the future Edward VII]
is going to you and I can't – and when I look at the baby things, and
feel I shall not be where every other mother is – and I ought to be and
can't – it makes me sick and almost frantic. Why in the world did you
manage to choose a time when we could not be with you? . . .

QUEEN VICTORIA (1819–1901)

from A Letter to the Countess of Bute, 28 January 1753

CONCEAL LEARNING

You should encourage your daughter to talk over with you what she reads; and as you are very capable of distinguishing, take care she does not mistake pert folly for wit and humour, or rhyme for poetry, which are the common errors of young people, and have a train of ill consequences. The second caution to be given her (and which is most absolutely necessary) is to conceal whatever learning she attains, with as much solicitude as she would hide crookedness or lameness: the parade of it can only serve to draw on her the envy, and consequently the most inveterate hatred, of all he and she fools, which will certainly be at least three parts in four her acquaintance. The use of knowledge in our sex, beside the amusement of solitude, is to moderate the passions, and learn to be contented with a small expense, which are the certain effects of a studious life: and it may be preferable even to that fame which men have engrossed to themselves, and will not suffer us to share. You will tell me I have not observed this rule myself; but you are mistaken: it is only inevitable accident that has given me any reputation that way. I have always carefully avoided it, and ever thought it a misfortune. The explanation of this paragraph would occasion a long digression, which I will not trouble you with, it being my present design only to say what I think useful for the instruction of my granddaghter, which I have much at heart. If she has the same inclination (I should say passion) for learning that I was born with, history, geography, and philosophy will furnish her with materials to pass away cheerfully a longer life that is allotted to mortals. I believe there are few heads capable of making Sir Isaac Newton's calculations, but the result of them is not difficult to be understood by a moderate capacity.

LADY MARY WORTLEY MONTAGU (1689–1762)

Children Do Not Know

Children do not know how their parents love them, and they never will till the grave closes over those parents, or till they have children of their own.

EDMUND VANCE COOKE (1866–1932)

from The Girlfriends' Guide to Surviving the First Year of Motherhood

Here's the truth: the birth of a baby is supposed to blow your schedule to bits, even if it nearly kills you and your mate. This is nature's way of making sure that we get our new priorities straight. The three most important things become, in this order:

1. The baby's health
2. The baby's comfort
3. The baby's parents survival (this is a very distant third)

VICKI IOVINE (1954–)

Instruction

Speak when ye're spoken tae,
Dae what ye're bidden,
Come when ye're ca'd,
And ye'll no be chidden

TRADITIONAL SCOTTISH RHYME

Which Day Are You?

Monday's child is fair of face,
Tuesday's child is full of grace,
Wednesday's child is full of woe,
Thursday's child has far to go.
Friday's child is loving and giving,
Saturday's child works hard for a living,
And the child that is born on the Sabbath, they say,
Is bonny and blithe and bright as the day.

TRADITIONAL

Babies

Babies wear their food and eat their clothes

JOHN DEAN (1770–)

Everything

Children find everything in nothing, men find nothing in everything.

GIACOMO LEOPARDI (1798–1837)

FAMILIES

The First Tooth

Through the house what busy joy,
Just because the infant boy
Has a tiny tooth to show!
I have got a double row,
All as white, and all as small;
Yet no one cares for mine at all.
He can but say but half a word,
Yet that single sound's preferred
To all the words that I can say
In the longest summer day.
He cannot walk, yet if he put
With mimic motion out his foot,
As if he thought he were advancing,
It's prized more than my best dancing.

CHARLES and MARY LAMB
(1775–1834) and (1764–1847)

The Second Child

You see I too
was second in order. Two.

Before you arrived
for a time I cried

nightly at the fattening, spelling the end
of our tight, well-tended

trio. The carefully scheduled bliss
of bath and bed – luxurious

brace of both to read a single book,
darting between us, her drinking-all-in, wee weighty look,

her finger-gesture toward some new developmental toy
or crystal bit of babble our post-crib nightcap, rehashed joy . . .

Now no rehash, littler miss,
of your airy imitation of her searing kiss:

down babyhood's brief corridor you disappear behind
her, the master dancer, your tutor in body and mind;

you not just child but sister. And while
she – so fierce, perversely proud – will be not child

but childhood's star, and pound the trail
and suffer in her art and, hell or high, refuse to fail

(you see it hurts, I love her so),
you will carelessly, sly, my sidelong darling, go

after: first toddling understudy, then patiently aslant
toward something other, invited by a glint I can't

discount. When your delighted eyes
dance at her back, assess the scene, I surmise

the end, and your means
to it. Like me –

for now I see, you showed me –
you'll be happy.

DEBORAH GARRISON (1965–)

Sister to Her Brother

What are little boys made of, made of?
What are little boys made of?
  Frogs and snails
  And puppy-dogs' tails,
That's what little boys are made of.

What are little girls made of, made of?
What are little girls made of?
  Sugar and spice
  And all things nice,
That's what little girls are made of.

ANONYMOUS

Jemima

There was a little girl, and she wore a little curl
  Right down the middle of her forehead
When she was good, she was very, very, good,
But when she was bad, she was horrid!

One day she went upstairs, while her parents, unawares,
  In the kitchen down below were occupied with meals,
And she stood upon her head, on her little truckle bed,
  And she then began hurraying with her heels.

Her mother heard the noise, and thought it was the boys
  A-playing at a combat in the attic,
But when she climbed the stair and saw Jemima there,
  She took and she did whip her most emphatic.

ANONYMOUS

Brother and Sister (1)

I cannot choose but think upon the time
    When our two lives grew like two buds that kiss
At lightest thrill from the bee's swinging chime,
    Because the one so near the other is.
He was the elder and a little man
    Of forty inches, bound to show no dread,
And I the girl that puppy-like now ran,
    Now lagged behind my brother's larger tread.
I held him wise, and when he talked to me
    Of snakes and birds, and which God loved the best,
I thought his knowledge marked the boundary
    Where men grew blind, though angels knew the rest.
If he said 'Hush!' I tried to hold my breath;
Wherever he said 'Come!' I stepped in faith.

Brother and Sister (2)

Long years have left their writing on my brow,
    But yet the freshness and the dew-fed beam
Of those young mornings are about me now,
    When we two wandered toward the far-off stream
With rod and line. Our basket held a store
    Baked for us only, and I thought with joy
That I should have my share, though he had more,
    Because he was the elder and a boy.
The firmaments of daisies since to me
    Have had those mornings in their opening eyes,
The bunched cowslip's pale transparency
    Carries that sunshine of sweet memories,
And wild-rose branches take their finest scent
From those blest hours of infantine content.

GEORGE ELIOT (1812–80)

The Twins

Not because of their beauty – though they are slender
as saplings of white cedar, and long as lilies –
not because of their delicate dancing step,
or their brown hair sideways blown like the manes of fillies –
it is not for their beauty that the crowd in the street
wavers like dry leaves around them on the wind.
It is the chord, the intricate unison
of one and one, strikes home to the watcher's mind.

How sweet is the double gesture, the mirror-answer;
same hand woven in same, like arm in arm.
Salt blood like tears freshens the crowd's dry veins,
and moving in its web of time and harm
the unloved heart asks, 'Where is my reply,
my kin, my answer? I am driven and alone.'
Their serene eyes seek nothing. They walk by.
They move into the future and are gone.

JUDITH WRIGHT (1915–2000)

Reminiscences

CHEERFUL COMFORTER

My earliest memory of all is a mad passion of rage at my elder brother John (on a visit to us likely from his grandfather's); in which my Father too figures though dimly, as a kind of cheerful comforter and soother. I had broken my little brown stool, by madly throwing it at my brother; and felt for perhaps the first time, the united pangs of Loss and of Remorse. I was perhaps hardly more than two years old; but can get no one to fix the date for me, though all is still quite legible for myself.

THOMAS CARLYLE (1795–1881)

A Terrible Infant

I recollect a nurse called Ann,
  Who carried me about the grass,
And one fine day a fine young man
  Came up, and kissed the pretty lass.
She did not make the least objection!
  Thinks I, '*Aha!*
  When I can talk I'll tell Mamma!'
—And that's my earliest recollection.

FREDERICK LOCKER (1821–95)

Gratitude

I remember . . . one noontime as I stood in the kitchen and watched my children eat peanut butter and jelly sandwiches. We were having a most unremarkable time on a nondescript day, in the midst of the most quotidian of routines. I hadn't censed the table, sprinkled the place mats with holy water, or uttered a sanctifying prayer over the Wonder bread. I wasn't feeling particularly 'spiritual'. But, heeding I don't know what prompting, I stopped abruptly in mid-bustle, or mid-woolgathering, and looked around me as if I were opening my eyes for the first time that day.

The entire room became luminous and so alive with movement that everything seemed suspended – yet pulsating – for an instant, like light waves. Intense joy swelled up inside me, and my immediate response was gratitude – gratitude for everything, every tiny thing in that space. The shelter of the room became a warm embrace; water flowing from the tap seemed a tremendous miracle; as my children became, for a moment, not my property or my charges or my tasks, but eternal beings of infinite singularity and complexity whom I would one day, in an age to come, apprehend in their splendid fullness.

HOLLY BRIDGES ELLIOT

Veneration

[A] grandmother must ever be loved and venerated, particularly one's mother's mother I always think.

QUEEN VICTORIA (1819–1901)

The Most Important Person

My grandmother . . . was the most important person to me throughout my childhood . . . She could speak French, German and Italian faultlessly, without the slightest trace of accent. She knew Shakespeare, Milton and the eighteenth century poets intimately. She could repeat the signs of the Zodiac and the names of the Nine Muses. She had a minute knowledge of English history according to the Whig tradition. French, German and Italian classics were familiar to her . . .

BERTRAND RUSSELL (1872–1970)

Maggie

We are a grandmother

MARGARET THATCHER (1925–)

from Good Morning, Merry Sunshine

GRANDPARENTS

I answered the door. They were standing there – my father with a camera in his hand, my mother carrying a bag full of presents – and they made their hellos to Susan and me. They walked into the living room. I don't think they were expecting to see Amanda yet, but she was on her back asleep in the carriage there.

They made sounds that I can only describe as animal-like when they saw her. The sight seemed to touch something so basic in them that the sounds came out; it was as if something had squeezed their hearts. I realized instantly that nothing I may ever accomplish in the world of work will possibly affect them in the way the sight of their granddaughter did.

They leaned close to her and talked to her, and there was none of the self-consciousness that sometimes marks our dealings with each other. It struck me that what they were going through was something very close to recapturing what they must have had when I was first born.

A man and woman have a child; for a period of time it is as if they are the only three people in the world. The closeness seems perfect. As the years go by, and the mother and father nurture the child and urge the child toward independence, a distance develops. When they want the best for the child, they automatically deprive themselves of the closeness that was there at first. In the case of my parents and myself, the distance – because of me – at times is great.

But suddenly here was Amanda Sue. And although they didn't express it verbally, I could tell that what my mother and father saw in her were some of the same things that they must have seen in me thirty-five years ago. In that baby they were seeing something they must have assumed they would never see again. They stared at her so fiercely; that had to be it, a sense of time and love recaptured.

BOB GREENE (1947–)

from Flush

DOGGY AFFECTION

But Flush was no longer the unschooled, untrained dog of Wimpole
Street days . . . The baby was set on his back and Flush had to trot
about with the baby pulling his ears. But he submitted with such
grace, only turning round, when his ears were pulled, 'to kiss the little
bare, dimpled feet', that, before three months had passed, this helpless,
weak, puling, muling lump had somehow come to prefer him, 'on the
whole' – so Mrs Browning said – to other people. And then, strangely
enough, Flush found that he returned the baby's affection. Did they
not share something in common – did not the baby somehow
resemble Flush in many ways? Did they not hold the same views, the
same tastes? For instance, in the matter of scenery. To Flush all scenery
was insipid. He had never, all these years, learnt to focus his eyes upon
mountains. When they took him to Vallombrosa all the splendours of
its woods had merely bored him. Now again, when the baby was a
few months old, they went on another of those long expeditions in
a travelling carriage. The baby lay on his nurse's lap; Flush sat on Mrs
Browning's knee. The carriage went on and on, painfully climbing the
heights of the Apennines. Mrs Browning was almost beside herself
with delight. She could scarcely tear herself from the window. She
could not find words enough in the whole of the English language to
express what she felt . . . the beauty of the Apennines brought words
to birth in such numbers that they positively crushed each other out
of existence. But the baby and Flush felt none of this stimulus, none
of this inadequacy. Both were silent. Flush drew 'in his head from the
window and didn't consider it worth looking at . . . He has a supreme
contempt for trees and hills or anything of that kind,' Mrs Browning
concluded. The carriage rumbled on. Flush slept and the baby slept.

VIRGINIA WOOLF (1882–1941)

Sonnet 17

Who will believe my verse in time to come,
If it were fill'd with your most high deserts?
Though yet, heaven knows, it is but as a tomb
Which hides your life and shows not half your
    parts.
If I could write the beauty of your eyes
And in fresh numbers number all your graces,
The age to come would say 'This poet lies;
Such heavenly touches ne'er touch'd earthly
    faces.'
So should my papers yellow'd with their age
Be scorn'd like old men of less truth than
    tongue,
And your true rights be term'd a poet's rage
And stretched metre of an antique song:
    But were some child of yours alive that time,
    You should live twice, in it and in my rime.

WILLIAM SHAKESPEARE (1564–1616)

A Human Calculation

If it had to be him
or them
let it be him.

If he had to choose between me
and them,
just one of them,
goodbye to me.

Take me,
take him,
God forbid them.

Blasphemous
back of the envelope:
we don't get
to subtract
or make trades.
Only to add
and clutch
at our number.

DEBORAH GARRISON (1965–)

Family

The older I get, the less religious faith I have. Instead, my faith is my family – and I suspect it's a faith that many women, irrespective of their spiritual beliefs, share. Bringing up children and holding a family together requires practising most, if not all, of the Christian tenets: putting others before yourself; being compassionate; acting for the greater good; being self-disciplined.

SANDRA PARSONS, *The Times*, 20 March 2008

from Nothing Is Lost

Nothing dies.
The cells pass on their secrets, we betray them
Unknowingly: in a freckle, in the way
We walk, recall some ancestor,
And Adam in the colour of our eyes.

Yes, on the face of the new born,
Before the soul has taken full possession,
There pass, as over a screen, in succession
The images of other beings:
Face after face looks out, and then is gone.

Nothing is lost, for all in love survive.
I lay my cheek against his sleeping limbs
To feel if he is warm, and touch in him
Those children whom no shawl could warm,
No arms, no grief, no longing could revive.

Thus what we see, or know,
Is only a tiny portion, at the best,
Of the life in which we share; an iceberg's crest
Our sunlit present, our partial sense,
With deep supporting multitudes below.

ANNE RIDLER (1912–2001)

A Truth

Families with babies and families without babies are sorry for each other.

E. W. HOWE

from Thicker than Water

I look so like these women who are now gone, the echo of my mother's flesh in my own, each finger wears her nail.

KATHRYN HARRISON

A World of
Their Own

The Land of Counterpane

When I was sick and lay a-bed,
I had two pillows at my head,
And all my toys beside me lay
To keep me happy all the day.

And sometimes for an hour or so
I watched my leaden soldiers go,
With different uniforms and drills,
among the bedclothes, through the hills.

And sometimes sent my ships in fleets
All up and down among the sheets;
Or brought my trees and houses out,
And planted cities all about.

I was the giant great and still
That sits upon the pillow-hill,
And sees before him, dale and plain,
The pleasant land of counterpane.

ROBERT LOUIS STEVENSON (1850–94)

from his Notebooks

Children in the wind – hair floating. tossing, a miniature of the agitated Trees, below which they play'd – the elder whirling for joy, the other in petticoats, a fat Baby, eddying half willingly, half by force of the Gust – driven backward, struggling forward – both drunk with the pleasure, both shouting their hymn of Joy.

SAMUEL TAYLOR COLERIDGE (1772–1834)

On Children

How dull our days, how lacking in surprise
Without these small epitomes of sin,
These flowers with their store of life within
And grave, appalling freshness in their eyes.

FRANCES CORNFORD (1886–1960)

Walking Away

It is eighteen years ago, almost to the day –
A sunny day with the leaves just turning,
The touch-lines new ruled – since I watched you play
Your first game of football, then, like a satellite
Wrenched from its orbit, go drifting away.

Behind a scatter of boys. I can see
You walking away from me towards the school
With the pathos of a half-fledged thing set free
Into a wilderness, the gait of one
Who finds no path where the path should be.

That hesitant figure, eddying away
Like a winged seed loosened from its parent stem,
Has something I never quite grasp to convey
About nature's give-and-take – the small, the
   scorching
Ordeals which fire one's irresolute day.

I have had worse partings, but none that so
Gnaws at my mind still. Perhaps it is roughly
Saying what God alone could perfectly show –
How selfhood begins with a walking away,
And love is proved in the letting go.

C. DAY LEWIS (1872–1938)

from A Writer's Diary

They have what no grown up has – that directness – chatter, chatter, chatter, on Ann goes, in a kind of world of her own, with its seals and dogs; happy because she's going to have cocoa tonight, and go blackberrying tomorrow.

The walls of her mind are all hung round with such bright vivid things, and she doesn't see what we see.

VIRGINIA WOOLF (1882–1941)

Feigned Courage

Horatio, of ideal courage vain,
Was flourishing in air his father's cane,
And, as the fumes of valour swelled his pate,
Now thought himself *this* hero, and now *that*;
'And now,' he cried, 'I will Achilles be;
My sword I brandish, see, the Trojans flee.
Now I'll be Hector when his angry blade
A lane through heaps of slaughtered Grecians made!
And now by deeds still braver I'll convince,
I am no less than Edward the Black Prince.
Give way, ye coward French!' As thus he spoke,
And aimed in fancy a sufficient stroke
To fix the fate of Cressy or Poictiers
(The nurse relates the hero's fate with tears);
He struck his milk-white hand against a nail,
Sees his own blood, and feels his courage fail.
Ah! where is now that boasted valour flown,
That in the tented field so late was shown?
Achilles weeps, great Hector hangs his head!
And the Black Prince goes whimpering to bed.

MARY LAMB (1764–1847)

Lullaby

Go to sleep, Mum,
I won't stop breathing
suddenly in the night.

Go to sleep. I won't
climb out of my cot and
tumble downstairs.

Mum, I won't swallow
the pills that doctor gave you or
put hairpins in electric
sockets, just go to sleep.

I won't cry
when you take me to school and leave me
I'll be happy with other children
my own age

Sleep, Mum, sleep.
I won't
fall in the pond, play with matches,
run under a lorry or even consider
sweets from strangers.

No, I won't
give you a lot of lip,
not like some.

I won't sniff glue,
fail my exams,
get myself/
my girlfriend pregnant.
I'll work hard and get a steady/
really worthwhile job.
I promise, I'll go to sleep.

I'll never forget
to drop in/phone/write
and if
I need any milk, I'll yell.

ROSEMARY NORMAN (1946–)

Exclusive

for my daughter

I lie on the beach, watching you
as you lie on the beach, memorizing you
against the time when you will not be with me:
your empurpled lips, swollen in the sun
and smooth as the inner lips of a shell;
your biscuit-gold skin, glazed and
faintly pitted, like the surface of a biscuit;
the serious knotted twine of your hair.
I have loved you instead of anyone else,
loved you as a way of loving no one else,
every separate grain of your body
building the god, as I built you within me,
a sealed world. What if from your lips
I had learned the love of other lips,
from your starred, gummed lashes the love of
other lashes, from your shut, quivering
eyes the love of other eyes,
from your body the bodies,
from your life the lives?
Today I see it is there to be learned from you:
to love what I do not own.

SHARON OLDS (1942–)

Children's Song

We live in our own world,
A world that is too small
For you to stoop and enter
Even on hands and knees,
The adult subterfuge.
And though you probe and pry
With analytic eye,
And eavesdrop all our talk
With an amused look,
You cannot find the centre
Where we dance, where we play,
Where life is still asleep
Under the closed flower,
Under the smooth shell
Of eggs in the cupped nest
That mock the faded blue
Of your remoter heaven.

R. S. THOMAS (1913–2000))

A Wish for My Children

On this doorstep I stand
year after year
to watch you going

and think: May you not
skin your knees. May you
not catch your fingers
in car doors. May
your hearts not break.

May tide and weather
wait for your coming

and may you grow strong
to break
all webs of my weaving.

EVANGELINE PATERSON (?–2000)

ACKNOWLEDGEMENTS

With thanks to all who have offered advice and help, including Keith Thomas, Amanda Craig, Kate Muir, Bel Mooney.

The publishers would like to acknowledge the following for permission to reproduce copyright material:

Extracts from the *Authorized Version of the Bible (The King James Bible)*, the rights of which are vested in the Crown, are reproduced by permission of the Crown's Patentee, Cambridge University Press.

Fleur Adcock: 'The Video' from *Poems 1960–2000* (2000), reprinted by permission of the publishers, Bloodaxe Books.

Yosana Akiko: 'Labour Pains' from *Women Poets of Japan 1973*, published by New Directions Publishing Corps.

A. S. Byatt: extract from 'A New Voice', from *Still Life* (Chatto and Windus, 1985), reprinted by permission of the author and Rogers, Coleridge and White Ltd.

Tina Cassidy: extract from *Birth, A History*, published by Chatto and Windus, 2007, reprinted by permission of Random House.

Kate Clanchy: 'Two Months Gone' from *New Born*, published by Picador, 2004, reprinted by permission of Pan Macmillan.

Merle Collins: 'Some Days, Mother' from *Rotten Pomerack* (Virago Press, 1992), reprinted by permission of the publishers, Little, Brown.

Frances Cornford: 'On Children' from *Selected Poems*, (Enitharmon Press, 1996).

Jeni Couzyn: 'Transformation' and 'Dawn' from *A Time to Be Born: Poems of Childbirth*, with illustrations by Clarie Weissman Wilks (Fire Lizard, 1999), reprinted by permission of the author.

Rachel Cusk: extracts from *A Life's Work: On Becoming a Mother* (Fourth Estate, 2001), © Rachel Cusk, 2001. Reproduced by permission. All rights reserved.

C. Day Lewis: 'Walking Away' from *The Complete Poems* of *C. Day Lewis* (Sinclair-Stevenson, 1992). Copyright © 1992 in this edition The Estate of C Day Lewis. Reprinted by permission of The Random House Group Ltd.

Maura Dooley: 'Freight' from *Sound Barrier: Poems 1982–2002* (2002), reprinted by permission of the publishers, Bloodaxe Books.

Rita Dove: 'Daystar' from *Thomas and Beulah* (Carnegie Mellon University Press, 1986), © 1986 by Rita Dove. Reprinted by permission of the author.

Margaret Drabble: from *The Millstone* (1965), published by Weidenfeld & Nicolson, a division of Orion Publishing Group. Reprinted by permission.

Carol Ann Duffy: from 'A Child's Sleep' from *Meeting Midnight* (1999), reprinted by permission of the publishers, Faber & Faber Ltd.

Lawrence Durrell: 'Cradle Song' from *The Tree of Idleness and Other Poems* (1955), reprinted by permission of the publishers, Faber & Faber Ltd.

Rebecca Eckler: extracts from *Knocked Up* (Villard Books, 2004), reprinted by permission of the author, whose other books include *Wiped!* and *Toddlers Gone Wild*.

Holly Bridges Elliot: from *Beholding God in Many Places* (Saint Mary's Press, 1993).

Sally Emerson: extract from *Separation* (Abacus 1993), reprinted by permission of Curtis Brown Ltd.

John Fuller: 'Birth Bells for Louisa' from *Now and for a Time*, published by Chatto &Windus. Reprinted by permission of The Random House Group Ltd.

Deborah Garrison: 'The Second Child' and 'A Human Calculation' from *The Second Child* (2008), reprinted by permission of the publishers, Bloodaxe Books.

Desmond Graham: 'Like a Fish Out of God's Hand' and 'She is Learning Her Hands' from *Milena Poems* (2004), reprinted by permission of the publishers, Flambard Press.

Bob Greene: extracts from *Good Morning, Merry Sunshine* (Atheneum, 1984), reprinted by permission of Sterling Lord Literistic, Inc.

Thom Gunn: 'Baby Song' from *Jack Straw's Castle* (1976), reprinted by permission of the publishers, Faber & Faber Ltd.

Robert Hayden: 'Those Winter Sundays' from *Complete Poems* (Liveright, 1996), reprinted by permission of W.W. Norton & Co. Inc.

Langston Hughes: 'Birth' from *The Collected Poems of Langston Hughes*, edited by Arnold Rampersad with David Roessel, Associate Editor, copyright © 1994 by The Estate of Langston Hughes. Used by permission of Alfred A. Knopf, a division of Random House, Inc.

Laurie Lee: extracts from *Two Women* (1983), published by André Deutsch, The Carlton Publishing Group.

John Lennon: 'Beautiful Boy' by permission of Shukat, Arrow, Hafer, Weber and Herbsman, L.L.P.

Philip Lerman: from *Dadditude, How a Real Man Became a Real Dad* (2007), reprinted by permission of the publishers, Perseus Books.

Sue Limb: extracts from *Love Forty* (Transworld, 1986).

Vicki Iovine: from *The Girlfriends' Guide to Surviving the First Year of Motherhood*, published by Perigee Books, 1997.

Audre Lorde: 'Now That I Am Forever With Child' from *Collected Poems* (1997), reprinted by permission of the publishers W.W. Norton & Co., Inc.

INDEX OF FIRST LINES

INDEX OF AUTHORS